ABO

John High is consummately an ~~~ smoked voice, the dead and the lost, the innocent and the doomed speak to us with an urgency we cannot forget. He writes as if his being were at stake, as if our being were at stake. Like St. Dominic in Fra Angelico's fresco, with all the world's "blue slime, pestilence, mosquitoes, rain" swirling around him, John High concentrates, in his own words, with the "clarity of the sun beating down." *Bloodline* maps a poetic line that shoots from the American South to Moscow, from zen aphorism to jazz-inspired improvisation, from suffering and redemption to suffering and redemption. —*Forrest Gander*

John High's poetry and prose bear witness to the tumultuous, sacred resonances of the word as flesh, of lives snared on mortality's hooks, and of love's tender and violent inconsistencies. With a remarkable wakefulness that is both concrete and transformational, High subtly weaves a world of parables and riddles reminiscent of Kafka and Jabès. We are continually thrown back upon a compassion that spills over the limits of division and separation, where shards of dreams and apparitions cast their lot across the paths of unwitting travelers and solitary monks. The complexity of High's profound caring for the other breathes through every line with a consistency of vision informed by an epic scope and feverish quest for renewal.
—*Charles Borkuis*

John High's poetry undulates, and yet silence eases its way through all the pages of *bloodline.* Redemption hovers, forgiveness is lost and found and often lost again. By way of fragmented preachings, tender insinuations and nursery rhymes gone batty, High's poetry connects us to each other by grappling with our doubts and the idea of ourselves as witnesses to our own salvation. A strange ellipsis underlies many of High's poems, as if the poems had been construed by penlight, in a desire to get the words down before they fell back again into blackness. —*Michelle Murphy*

These poems resemble Tarkovsky's slow pans across a winter landscape. Here are allegories of absent presences, revelations delivered by a dangerous angel. High's words are heavy, but seem to hang, miraculously redeemed, in mid-air.
—*Andrew Joron*

Of the choices possible to a poet John High has chosen the most difficult [in *Ceremonies*]: out of loss and absence and despair to make a new world in a new language, to come as close as we can come to apprehending God without attributes, to find a pure place to try to be human in. . . . —*William Dickey*

John High's poems [in *Ceremonies*] move me by their authenticity, their urgent and deep emotional content. . . . They had to be poems. Moving in and by image and intuition, they'd discover, as they go, the shapes and patterns by which thoughts, concepts, and states of feeling sing themselves forth. —*Denise Levertov*

In *the lives of thomas,* John High re-imagines one version of Southern myth-making and tale-telling as a gnostic text, restoring to some of the fundamental images in

American culture an expressive power obscured through years of commercial trivialization and aesthetic distrust. If in its improvisatory order, its revelation of profundity in pop themes, and its swiftly shifting counterpoint there is something jazz-like in High's writing, its language also resembles an old-time preacher's, cajoling, imploring, lamenting, consoling, and witnessing, visionary and exact. This is important work, in search of the tracks even loss and death leave. —*Peter Weltner*

Ghosted. Jazzed. A delta poem-noir complete with alligator shoes, mattress out back, culpable deaths and a doppelganger to tell it to. (Thus) *the lives of thomas* digress through veiled archetypal passages: "So go out to the roads, bring those who you find they'll say." This transcript of lies, stolen between lives, slips through the hard planes of time into an undisclosed surround. *The lives of thomas*, which is not a story, adjusts, as an eye to the available light. —*C.D. Wright*

John High's writing has an element of music, sometimes a story, in which sensual detail is like "the changes and shifts of dream that go unnoticed in gesture."
—*Leslie Scalapino*

Forms and landscapes as in the paintings of Fairfield Porter—soft light, Motion—but now underscored in positive black, the thoughts themselves, like those of the gnostic Thomas. . . . —*Fanny Howe*

The Sasha Poems is contemplative poetry of the highest order. . . . The sentence by sentence run of these moving prose poems will hold you in its gentle grasp for a long while, even after you've stopped reading. John High has here mined his soul for a poetry that will awaken yours. —*Norman Fischer*

Through brief lyrics, prose poems, and long narratives, John High has been steadily refining a hybrid poetical form which is uniquely his own. —*Jim Leftwich*

. . . brilliant journeys into childhood, archetypal presences, and grief. . . . John High's work is vast, intimate, violent, comforting, and incredibly aware of what it means to BE in the world. —*Susan Smith Nash*

John High's expansive opus, *The Desire Notebooks,* pulsates with fullness and loss. It's always startling to find yourself close to someone whose vibrant voice responds to every nuance of the breathing world, whose sentient experience is so awake that you find yourself awakened. This work roves through rituals of experience and imagination, taking us there. —*Frances Mayes*

{*The Desire Notebooks* is a] beautiful book; luminous, mysterious, hypnotic.
—*Carole Maso*

[In *The Desire Notebooks*] John High calibrates history and modernity, poetry and prose, earnest letter and purposeful mistranslation, language and narrative, in one grand masterwork. —*Leonard Schwartz*

bloodline

BY JOHN HIGH

POETRY

Ceremonies

Sometimes Survival

the lives of thomas—episodes and prayers

along her thighs
(selected poems in Russian, trans. Nina Iskrenko)

The Sasha Poems

The Desire Notebooks

TRANSLATOR

Blue Vitriol by Aleksei Parshchikov
(with Michael Palmer and Michael Molner)

The Right to Err:
Selected Poems of Nina Iskrenko
(with Patrick Henry and Katya Olmsted)

The Inconvertible Sky by Ivan Zhdanov
(with Patrick Henry)

EDITOR

Crossing Centuries: The New Generation in Russian Poetry
(with Vitaly Chernetsky, Thomas Epstein, Lyn Hejinian, Patrick Henry,
Gerald Janecek, Laura Weeks, and others)

john high

bloodline

selected writings

Talisman House, Publishers
Jersey City, New Jersey

Published by
Talisman House, Publishers
P.O. Box 3157
Jersey City, New Jersey 07303-3157

Manufactured in the United Sates of America
Printed on acid-free paper

LIBRARY OF CONGRESS CATALOGUING-IN-PUBLICATION DATA

High, John Alexander.
    Bloodline : selected writings / John High.
    p. cm.
    ISBN 1-58498-024-9 (acid-free paper) — ISBN 1-58498-025-7 (pbk. : acid-free
    paper)
    I. Title.

PS3558.I3625 A6 2001
811'.54--dc21

2001052244

ACKNOWLEDGMENTS

A special thanks to Kathleen Savino and Erin Tribble
for their invaluable help in making this book possible.

Selections from *Ceremonies* (1984)
are reprinted by permission of the publisher, Concourse Press.

Selections from *The Desire Notebooks* (1999)
are reprinted by permission of the publisher, Sputen Duyvil.

to Sasha
High
FroM PaPa JohN
For Sasha High
FroM FroM FroM John
PaP High High John Papa High
John Pap

"He who lives in forgetfulness,
dies in a dream."

You can't clean blood with blood, Papa.

CONTENTS

from *The Sasha Poems*

from *Ceremonies*

from *the lives of thomas: episodes & prayers*

from *The Desire Notebooks*

from *Ravage*

from THE SASHA POEMS:
(a book of fables) (1997)

Why do you think this is your book, Sasha?
Because I am writing it, papa.

"*the small boats*," #1

—*for katya olmsted*

There are things you will remember, father. You think of me
as but a child now, yet the human leaves on the water express
another. Sideways, the reflections from the broken mirror by the
lake. How even I can take the longest of your fingers. Being,
belonging then. This love, and the way the death of another in the
other dream haunts you still. Fine-tuned grass, yellowed by the
white hillside, the moon so blue, chilled. Porcupines & grasshoppers
in the weeds. So is the curiosity of your own face, also a child's.
Consciousness but a leaf you saw when you left Russia & stood by the
station near the poet's house. The sadness you will remember too,
though when you read my letter in twenty-five years I will be in
that country, as you have been. Your slippery mind & the girls
laughing in the university, calling you — *professor.* Mother was
always more than two people. Coming to terms with your own life,
an American lost in America because there is no longer an America.
Even the monks told you this on the train before our birth, thumbing
through the book when you first saw the burnt angel. Wasps & bees

& yellow-jackets swarming behind us today! Blackberry pies rippled across the vine. Yet you are shivering & hungry. Why? The monks in the story only reflections, these green pods in the wooden bowl behind the shade. So you abandoned the monastery — this, *here,* is your life. Beside me. At a station by our lake. There will be snow, too. Therefore be at peace with me. I have done you no harm. Nor has this heroism & striving. These small fishing boats!

"*the first letter,*" #2

—for lori lubeski

The child chose this shape despite my own doubts, these
reckonings. . . . For this reason, not the one you expected, we awoke
with her sleeping on my arm in the rain after hearing a mother's
voice in the road. There are those who listen to this music and those
who color its sound. Choral chant, what began as a dream unsayable:
Cock a doodle doo, my dame has lost her shoe. . . . The hazel-gray of the
father's eyes closing as the garbage trucks arrived by the river. But
what does the hair mean? Please do not say it. Her life will begin
here, again. The letters on the table, the sky burning outside & this
image that sends the eyes walking down a road. The difference is
Emphasis. You say child, God says Another, and St. Francis is
whistling to the almond tree — knock upon yourself as upon a door.
An angel was once in this room. Ezekiel healed him. His arms aflame
yet calm as the sun we imagine. We spoke of the apple blossom on
the edge of a cup of coffee. I doubted my own sincerity seeing the
snows of siberia, hearing of the loss of our sister. . . . An animal appears,
a rock falls, and suddenly there is the letter S. The risk is not a loss
of meaning, but the ghosted quest is this journey of a life. What are
the red-leaved trees saying? Where does the wind go? O monk of
desire, why have you abandoned us? We find all of these voices.
Peach blossom then & the mediation of hours. Waking up in the
prayer. She was the one who sent the eyes walking. The child's
message was simple enough.

"all the king's men," #4

—for jim leftwich

Her hand revealed a humpty-dumpty smallness, something
he had not witnessed before. Egg-shells, splintered stones, this
tossed-aside yet persistent dreaming. A child, the father's child,
and there she stood at the corner with three rickety dolls, a toy fire
truck, the white & black teddy bears by a windmill. Why meditate
on that which eludes the imagination, or on that which is gone? the
ghost had said. The first word came in drunkenness before she was
born. The voice itself singing in the uterus & the father had stepped
back, astonished for the first time absent of any fear or loneliness.
A dog howling on the edge of Time. Shank blue leaves on the trees &
the child took his hand, pointed toward the curtainless window
looking out on the Kremlin. She counted all the king's faces & all the
king's men & every part of her face began to shine. A first word,
father. The legs of the chair prancing. A peach lying on the floor by
the graffitied wall and suddenly all of the toys alive again!

She was the one who showed the monks here, back to this road.
And he had stumbled into this plain too, unknowingly. Once upon a
time. Before & after the great fall. Naturally, the road had become a
speech & the speech spooked him & all but one of the monks who
escorted the child.

And now she was smiling. So childish, papa. You are so
childish. As he walked toward the door. And once again we ask,
could you with certainty object to these buckles on our shoes!

"*a map, a goose & a fairy tale,*" #6

—for vladimir druk

The paper in her hand, no it was a book she was carrying through the sparkling & overgrown field. The ghosts of the geese began their squaking with the faint light of sunrise. But then, the child had uttered such even before her birth, at first in a foreign tongue the father recognized but didn't truly understand. Obliterated clouds & stars manifesting. Heads of lettuce, the brown frogs & roasted walnuts from the sun. Orpheus not singing. Onions rolling across the path as the morning continued. Old soul! the poet called to them, seeing only a photograph of the child in his dream. Ezekiel, the boldest, refrained from naming our vision. Thus the monks traveled on toward evening. Come, and I will return your poetry, the child sighed after sipping from the creek & glancing toward a sky full of blackbirds & sparrows. The queen of hearts then made some tarts and not one of the sojourners was hungry.

These sparrows no one beckons! The angel picked a muffler from the water, content to mimic the day. If those who lead you say — Look the Kingdom, it is in the sky — then the birds of the sky will get there first, the angel heckled as a possum scampered by. Since its own wings were burnt, the angel again exploded in flames. Though the mud itself was cool on our toes. The field presently shrouded in an early autumn fog as a turtle turned in the bush. If the child had known the flowers, she would have named them too in our eternalistic pathos. . . . Can you translate the silence, papa? she next inquired.

This the origin of many tests. O gray hummingbird! A birth meandering along the road. So many joys no one had mentioned to the father before now. *Jack be nimble, Jack be quick.* She laid the pages down on the ground & called it a book. The ants & approaching squirrels called it a diary.

This will be my book, papa.

"*popsickles & gasoline*," #10

—*for nina iskrenko's birthday memorial*

There is no measuring with the body. A child. . . a thread of purple yarn, the closing door when I left the other country. *That which you do not bring forth will destroy you*. What did a city mean, this place I was going? One, two, buckle my shoe! See this road — my girl lying in the grass, praying by an abandoned gas station, the pigeons fluttering about the curb. Some parts of our life are real. Stirring about the pantry with Peter Pan, cooking eggs in a tub of oil. . . . A photograph of three years then, starting again — the tears behind the taut skin of our wandering sister as the train hovered in the last station. Pat-a-cake, pat-a-cake, baker's man. Good-bye, sister! In the house a bar of soap, a human face, the water in the monks' jar. Together the child & I will leave here, since like St. Anthony, we refuse to go it alone. Orpheus on the balcony beckoning to the fire trucks in the morning brightness. Why only yesterday at the cemetery, I lost my nerve! Or as the poet said, *I can resist everything except temptation*. We will become another person, that person. Reading Ecclesiastes & O dear what can the matter be. A sky populated with migrating pink birds. Such pinkness! Three, four, shut the door, papa. . . . Overlooked in the sparse hives I found her naked doll. The child giggling afterwards, our mothers dancing with the zzzz of the bumble bee. I counted out our change. For if you can do the same thing in the exact way & time everyday, you can save the world. O, this later scene of blood-soil, poppy-seed bagels, the ghost sculpting time with popsickles. Five, six, pick up the sticks! Eternity's hostage, an act for the sun of our day. Awakening in a five room garage where all of the furniture rises up one night & says, I love you. Good-bye. Good-bye, sister. This day, more than any other, we love you.

"*our dream of you,*" #16

—for michelle murphy

Naming of the past, or this radiance in the sky where the crows
were again crowding. The ducks want someone to take care of them,
papa. . . . The blackbirds calling in the bush & our conviction to carry
on conflicted by the fatigue of legs, by her father's constant chatter in
an oblique light. The man folded the sheet of their tent into four
corners. Knowledge & more bees & mosquitoes & the quotes from the
mute monk in the squirrel's eyes. Though the man could not, or
refused, to make them tea this morning. As if our existence alone
might pull the dead one from the road, or as if the acorns were a map
& summary of the virgin life to come. How did she first come to this
apple tree?

The crows constant change as the weather took its various
shapes & faces among the others. Your shelters for the poor. Pine
& feathers crushed beneath the feet of the passersby. St. Francis
meandering into a void of women in prayer just as a mother's body
once shrouded a landscape of sun & moon & no fear. Transformation
of a deserted cottage as the dead one now enters. A burning angel again
falling to earth & these nomads — yes, the man growing younger as
the child ages. *Mystery worthy of mysteries*, why do the turtles follow us?
She kicks the rusted pipe. The world begs for quiet. As if these two
figures alone touch our dream of you.

"*venice dream*," #17

—for andrew joron

The tepid ghost of shadows on the floor, the diary of a mother.
The monks had at last touched him. Wandering through the hillside he
sensed this presence. When the sparrows began to flutter. In the
old cottage the writers had gathered & though not embracing
us, the father had not disturbed their conversation. Window in the
clouds, willows in the morning. The chorus opened its voice & in this
he listened. A stone road gradually tapered off into woods, then a
burst into the meadow, and the man had found himself traipsing
through these forgotten hills alone, without the child or angel.
Sparrows & white crows & ducks! A coughing sound from the door
but he had not hesitated to enter since the fear & loneliness had
exhausted him. They were the great writers, the ones he had read
since his own childhood, and they were lamenting. For the Book.
Their talk huddled in corners & darkness. A sheet on the solitary
cot, soiled & dusty. What words had once been on these shelves?
A discarded lamp shade, the man carried it into the candle-lit room
where Shakespeare & Dante were whispering: *See the cow and that
one goat as memory and desire.* Outside he saw nothing, yet this was
the shy one talking, standing back from the others. Orchestrated
light filtering from the window & a silent desire. Orchestrated light
filtered from the window and a silence resonated while the other
poets spoke a commentary on the quiet night and their own absence
of single lines in one miraculous book. As if all they had written
could be reduced to one line for one year in each of the centuries of
their lives.

Those who once lived here gone now. Across the yard & over
the fence, a small goat roamed. The monks had at last heard him,
but the man was frightened by the names — Rilke & Mandelstam,
Goethe & Dickinson, Lorca & all those who travel with us. . . . There
were too many hills leading back to the road where he had lost the
child, bade the angel farewell. As if welcoming back the past. Yet this,
too, was still to come in our dream. When the two walked together &
not alone. Because the ghost of shadows had entered him by way of a
diary. His daughter's diary. Her fractured note on Ezra Pound & the
grave in Venice. Though he had found it, she would remember.

In this way we began again in search of the Book.

"the end of the world," #18

—for don hilla

The waterfall came down into the mouths of the gulls! They
had walked for hours, the father & child alone, and when the girl
recognized the gulls she heard a horrific cry. . . . The man, drunk &
unshaven, squatted in the late afternoon sun, oblivious to the water,
the gulls, the stark rasps of quotations on the small lake. The child
moved freely through his muteness, questioning none of it as history
would become her own telling of suns. Caterpillars & crickets on the
bank, in the insects & roads, in our blood & in our dying. Our
one-eyed raccoon across the ridge, mocking the world. Somewhere
in the other expanse, on another day, Ezekiel nudged the shoulder of
the man when he was himself only a boy, deaf & dumb — pointing to
the lupine of another field where burning white stones were covered
in thick frost & obliterated his ignorance. The monks understood the
death of the snow & thus had followed the two here today, many
years later, to this waterfall, by a lake full of tenacious birds —
crossing the chaos of time. . . . Since what you come to see, the blind one
admonished, you come to believe. And this is without a name.

Let me guess, you see our mother again? the girl quizzically
asked, herself witnessing the hues of madness, of an elm on the ridge
of what we once called fable. She then ran to the shore of rocks
under the fall, her fingers swimming in the foam — & later talking to
Orpheus too, since he had trailed her to the lake's edge & popped his
head from the spray, spying on her. The mountain without a name &
purpose here. Nothing. We're on slippery grass, everywhere we
turn, the poet told her. Your star is yet to be born.

Why have you come? She tossed crumbs from her pocket into his gushing mouth. The ducks — & these forlorn gulls who were jealous & frantic — beckoned their own mouths toward the child & gathered around. What happened to my father that he should be so distracted by the cries of God. . .

The sun sets.
The moon rises.

And suddenly, it is tomorrow again!

I do not need your divinity or lies.

When I lost you, I didn't know who I was. . . . the father at last answered as the one-eyed raccoon found its way to the water where we were all anxiously waiting.

The evening you escaped the world they (those who are outside us) lamented, Orpheus cawed as the frogs croaked & the ducks quacked & the gulls crooned out to the orphaned gods. Ezekiel then took his tin cup & scooped it across the surface of rocks. Finally, finally we are all together! the monk sighed, motioning to the animals — and this is when the child saw him as a boy, her father squatting barefoot in the snow, a deaf & dumb one, & on the flat plains of siberia, watching the rustling & leaves & the smoke rising in his nose & in his arms like the birch trees, this beginning, or burning, like the bone stones & like the snows & the end of the world dancing & traipsing our mundane naming of Time. The heathen cry out in hell. She took the razor from her father's bag & while shoving away the others, slowly began to shave the man's face.

"fools in paradise," #19

—for aleksei parshchikov

The moon had been shining for three days. O woman in the
moon! she whispered under the shell. A pelican, a crow, a goose,
and a rainbow. Still, the child did not find this language difficult.
Though at times she wished for a clock, a way to remember the
things that didn't occur. The pale white cliffs overhead. Their faces
staring out of the fog. Our gray-winged pelicans. Her father's
scribbling. Compelled by the air unfolding in a bird's flight &
redemption. She saw a photo once, one of a priest & one who had not
yet been forgiven. The atrocity of that face. Her father self-obsessed
& proud in the photo. Once heard, the waves languished in sound.
The child becoming a child & if only she'd been granted a mediation
of speech this morning. Lazy papa! she cried. Cows & goats praying
on the hillside & all you do is. . . . Why could Orpheus not be among us
here? She might call this shore home today. Randomly — our sea — &
all of this water! Wear you a hat or wear you a crown! Hermes
cawed. Sea seeing sea seen. The monks breathing in the grass &
leaves & watermelons & searching beyond the graves. Why so many
graves when you marry a child? The path against the real. Be you a
hat or a crown!

Against the reef of jetty, black gulls. Beside you, our pelican, a
crow, a goose, and a rainbow. Still, she did not find the orphaned
god. Today. Instead she picked up a yellow bucket washed up on the
beach, filled it with pebbles & sand from the sea. Come & play!
She tickled herself. All that goes up must surely come down.
Hermes kisses her hand. O, how many feet are walking here? A
diamond in the sky. She lets the sand shift in her toes & watches the

waves — these blood lizards & pigeons & cliffs & hills that approach us. A whale! she hollers now. Come & play! A diary when the moon has been shining for three days! Our past is a simple house. When occupied.

Here. Walk in it, the sun. The reef of jellyfish. Sneaker waves & a ghost talking in a book. Are you frightened? There, by the crow. White daisies in the weed, you my soul. . . . And now, a pelican & crow beside us, like husband & wife. As if God.

"fables of hell," #20

—for cydney chadwick

No longer part of the dream the father began the day in
memory. There, the flight of the bird & the moon collided. The
child's stories like lyrical pieces of fruit in the basket resting by the
water. The convincing parable is the unopened one, the dead one
observed — seeing the child's diary among the stones — and then she
spoke languidly of the lost sparrows masquerading in the guises of
truth. Clowns & lunatics roaming as the breeze it came home again.
If the man had been lost, then the crisp rain & huge expanse of
memory would not have found him here — not even here, on the bank
of this river, chewing a piece of white bark from the oak. . . . Since time
is an entity like you or I, he told the child after finding this cool
shade & slice of being. The moon looked out of the man & once more,
no terror as the sky came down & the apples were green, edible. The
blossoms of the apple like apple blossoms never eaten. And O this
blue — & a rose of darkness — these locusts & snails marching!

No, the apple's sour, the child replied. But our monks are lost
on the hillside, shall we help them, papa? The music of her fingers
on the stones! Only a child could speak it, imagine the monks
through the smoke of fish frying on the fire. He wondered in
amazement how she'd led them from the sea, inward again, toward
this nameless river by the sea? The confession of stones is an
unheard one.

We will search the invisible God, the dead sighed as Orpheus
kneeled on the bank. . . . Dancing later in the tan leaves, the child would
know & feel the layers of her mother's face simply by the acts of

15

courage & retreat & salt on the edge of her tongue — these butterflies swarming about the face & the monks tumbling down the hill to greet her in merriment! What would a confession entail if the apple seeds were to speak into silence?

I want a yellow bicycle! she squealed. As if she were indeed a child and this was no parable! Then night, and more nightfalls. Elephants riding across the great deserts, Orpheus hooted, clasping my hand. . . .

The child's grin made confusion tangible, so the man abandoned this memory. She wanted milk in the evening, so he approached a farmer wandering on the road, listening to another's soul. The farmer had pointed them in this direction, so as if taking his own hand & placing a slice of salted fish on the inside of his palm, the girl whispered — will we discover our other face? All praise falleth short . . . do not mourn on the dead. A piper here, and even this occasion pleased us.

The shining smell of jasmine! *Soon people will speak of silence as a fable.* Orpheus showed his teeth & in this, mirrored another of her fathers — peeking under the stone himself, beside her now. . . . The smoke & fish & living, are they not the same, papa?

Identity came in the night when no one was looking.

"odd—shaped tomatoes," #24

—for evgenii bunimovich

The trail about the river appeared fragmented. Tired deer eyes gleaming in the shade as they crossed a cluster of pine. By evening the stars, too, would be vanquished, yet now they sat in the sky as oblivious to these two figures walking as they were to the sky itself. When the child asked him for fish, her laughter seemed to split his doubt down the middle, like a tree. Little Miss Muffet running in the forest today. The inclination & mood of squirrels. The foliage so purple, smelling of dove shit.

When the child asked him for bread, the guardian of love, the one the two searched for, emerged along the path. A mere shadow of an old woman wearing no shoes. These odd-shaped tomatoes the child picked that morning from the vine: lush, red, parabolic. When she asked the father for wind, most of her life was remembered without effort by her, the father, or the guardian before them on the path. Since the child had found the wind under a haystack.

Ghosted and alive we read these lines in which the deer continue, the mother had written before her birth, meticulously writing out the words of the first monk, who later still would become her guide. While the landscape shifted & the letters breathed a perfect calm in the breeze, the trees, the road, and the signs. This absence of automobiles, convenience stores, bright painted buildings. . . . Then the ferrets, roads, & roses. Yellow ones this time. Dear You & Mother, the child whispered, for if it had been written in flesh, she was determined to commit it to heart. The child did not care why.

The night departed & the two looked at the stars & then felt
completely at peace with one another. As they traversed the
meadow, the wooden crosses opened up before them. The tinted
leaves of the trees, how can the sky be so musical? She reached for
the father's hand to steady her own footsteps. Her hand, the
brightest one there, held the beauty of everything which might
occur, just as his own childhood contained this stretch of footsteps to
the snow, the monks, this reckoning. Our friends will help you, papa.
Come blow your horn! A black-stoned house, one of river stones.
Butterflies & raisins in the palm. She fetched a pail of water.
Because that's what she wanted. No longer nervous beside him. She
sung him a nursery rhyme. Scarecrows & crows. Silence, the trade
off of faces in the wood. The trail growing more narrow & the silence
now spoken.

When she asked him for fish.
When the child asked him for bread.
When she asked the father for wind.

Each of the monks, who had once been her father, began to
chuckle as the sheep gathered around, fast asleep. Since they too had
met the Guardian in this way.

18

"epiphany," #25

—for ed foster

In all manner blessed, though the meaning of the fields eluded
the man until now. The truth of their praise for this persistence in
the early morning walks. A memory vanishing & emerging in the
figure of monks on the ridge where, in the poet's tongue, giant ant-
eaters were always waiting. Bits of tangerine, flakes of fruit
dropping in the weeds. This manna from man. He wanted to wash
the child's feet, but he was afraid that she may still be hungry and
that they should keep moving. . . . Finding the refused questions in the
pages & in the hands. It was a journey into the words, no matter
how hard the man attempted to rationalize this time: *passion, epiphany*
redemption. incarnation. Is this our truth, spontaneous &
obsequious? the dead one demanded. Holiness camping by the
rivers, along the roads & in the petals of grass. He imagined a
window of a house in which life might be normal. And the child felt
no need to understand this. The shape of her head, itself like a small
cup — his own desire masquerading as sadness. The curious sighting
of a raven & helicopter overhead. While walking he dreamed again
of the poet's walk, memorizing the lines of a condemned poetry,
though in the end, the dictators had not vanquished the voice or won
our silence.

Why do we forget love at that very moment when we most
embrace it? he had asked the dead one, just as she had inquired that
morning — Do you see the doves in the margins of the diary? The
wise man in the parable simply lent the three sons another camel in
order that they might fulfill their father's prophecy & enter the
desert, Hermes interrupted. Only seventeen camels to divide equally

among the three & in this manner the wise one had solved the riddle
of his sons' greed.

All our days are bright & clear! O witness what we cherish!
This is where we belong, the child said now, lifting a stone from the
earth. Once more, the memory of sharp pieces of rice paper cutting
his hand when the monks discovered her. You will keep on walking,
Ezekiel instructed. If I were to ask you for fish, would you give me a
snake?

As a boy he had loved the nursery rhymes. They had
comforted his exile in the years of wandering with our terrible angel.
So this word, the flower of it, how the child repeated the sound over
& over — like a moon was inside her mouth & the spoon of it had
become a sky — brought the ghost nearer. The father sat her down
& pulled her toes, told her of the desert fathers and the child's first
encounter with solitude among the angels.

But if the tree is sad, will it bring bad fruit? she asked, tasting
the tangerine.

Spontaneous in this manner, so they continued in the book.
The vision more obstructed by objects than these apparitions. We
were both the ghost in the shade & the shade.

"or zebras perhaps," #32

—for cole swensen

The long line of gray-white fences meandered into the meadow
as if there were animals here: unicorns, bears, great-toothed tigers &
even zebras perhaps. The child skipped through the forest after
seeing the vision. She was whistling for her mother, but she wasn't
sure why. When the father reached the cemetery, she saw him lean
against the stone, hand reaching out & over as if to embrace the soil
beneath it. . . . Specific ghosts are not real ghosts, Ezekiel then uttered,
waving to the raven & crow that alighted by the father's foot. So
many things had gone astray, yet each day had brought them closer
to the joy she could not speak. Alpha. Omega. This moment as they
stared at the mustard-seeds planted about the horizon. Straw in the
stable, the three wise ones, the camel who spoke like a woman.
These images which came to the child as she studied the old man's
gesture. Some years ago, the father withstood the same experience
& so now, he would repeat it. Our life depended on a meaning
obvious in the birds' posture. O where, O where can my little . . . the
mother was cooing now, and it was now that the two witnessed the
face together: the collapsing silence of it spread as the girl dashed
forward, wandering for an hour in the sun. They had come home.
Seeing a bone of an eagle in the gold-bladed grass. And that bone,
too, seeing.

"*turnips & onions*," #33

—for fanny howe

When everything is here right now, why do you wait to be
happy? the dead one asked as the father watched the deaf horse &
donkey trot leisurely into view. That which you are looking for has
already found you! the monks then chimed in. . . . Thousands of
cockroaches spilling out of the ground where the slant of sun collided
at his feet. The child grinned sheepish & alone, sensing this was our
moment of truth. Why is no one crying? she herself inquired,
smiling afterwards as the rays hit the edge of the shed's roof. A
slight breeze. Hickory, dickery. . . . St. Francis is a funny one! the elder-
monk whined & pined, staring at our heroine in disbelief. Why
disbelief? Because she was barefoot & lovely & because she was
whistling having now scooped her father's hand to her eyebrows.
The mushrooms & deep allusions of autumn! These shifting oranges
& reds in the mulberry & madrone leaves. Hey Zeus. Everyday I see
the birds on the horizon, the dead one went on, chattering as she
reached for a piece of tobacco from her shell. The oval shell echoing
the splendor of Oz as the donkey lies down beneath the legs of the
horse & the frogs croak in rapture. . . . A handsome face, you have a
handsome face, Ezekiel! The girl sighs, almost ecstatic. She
darts toward the white turnips & onions remaining in the field.
They'll pass like pieces of floating rain. Her mother not at all
surprised as she watches this. But who will translate our memory
into the morning? The moon so fantastic as the turtles hurrrry their
way toward her. Orpheus, too, tiptoeing around the almond tree
since this is love. If you bring a message, why don't you stay for
tea? one might have asked. Or, as the dead one says — please try not
to forget. The masks alive. The child shuffling past poor Francis &

the others. . . . buzzing — O world, if you contain our silence, where will it grow?

"clouds & lunatics," #34

—for tom leaver

Orpheus crawled across the road. . . . The monks' laughter
refracted in the trees & curious rain. The child, however, was no
longer enticed by the clouds or the way the voices began this panorama
of evenings. The confession of stones is a prayer too, Ezekiel noted,
eyeing the poet's hands. Events & snails beside Orpheus, as if they
were all crossing the road together. The child washed her own & the
father's clothes in the river. By afternoon, the swan departed and his
shirts had dried on a willow branch. And now she saw him again,
crawling in the middle of the road. . . . What are you doing, papa?
Then there was this piper who played his pipe somewhere in the forest.
But where will we go? The flight of a bumble bee as the sun & moon
converse & combine & come back into vision. The father & child hug
each other too, and later she will tell him the diary has no name. Why
won't you pronounce our mother's name, papa? Grace. There. He
finally said it. Somewhere in the pose, a woman. There on the bank,
she heard the birch trees talking. The angel hiding in the azure—
colored leaves. What can any confession entail as the monks collect
their things, garner Orpheus on their shoulders and continue down the
road? In order to get out of it, he would have to go inside, since you
can't stop a man from transformation. You can't stop a man from
transforming himself.

"the same road," #38

— for peter weltner & atticas carr

Something delicate witnessed, transition notes. Etches in the
road, faint echoes from a horn of another hillside. The man was
unsure while welcoming the evening fire. If there had been rain,
the child's coughing would have reminded him of himself as a boy &
walking by morning in the strange amazement of trees left in the
tracks of a mother. What becomes of your dreams no longer matters,
Mika burped — the handless monk entering the field to pick the moist
poppy seeds. A cat slowly meandered past the other monks as the
girl kissed the boo-boo on her knee. It was like this. She healed
herself today, and even the dead one found it pleasing. The father
had followed the trail without trepidation after sensing the dove
float into a lavender mist. The condensed moments of change as the
bird flew skyward. If there had been snow the man would have
remembered & then forgotten again his own transformation as a child
— the epiphany in the white-haired moss & the chanting, like smoke,
lifting from the siberian wilderness. You have been walking the same
road all of your life. This is your home & renunciation, Dogen
observed, counting the ruby-throated humming birds three times. A
home, this monastery by the fire, these pine needles & porcupines &
the narrow gorge the father & child traversed together to find a night.
One mouse in the field, too. One snake. A flock of sooty terns. Stag
beetles. The holy trees beckoning as the invisible story slips with the
gestures of the monks' eyes. Papa, she whispered, again hearing the
flight. Papa. . . have all of these birds come to see me?

"after 40 days & 40 nights," #40

—for yuri arabov

. . . so who will move beyond the words? Dogen asked, squinting
at the young monk pulling the chair & then sitting himself on the
earth. This is our final hour & we know no other! Mika at last burst
into tears. The air thick in fog, in the residue of rain — these ants
scuttling without frenzy. The gulls' bodies swooping through the air,
their massive wings leaving traces of scarred clouds & shadow behind
them. After the sacrifice of so many hours walking, the dead too,
wanted to sit, so they joined the monk by the ruins. The girl's senses
alive & tingling as she followed the trail of water. In our panic we
knew this knowledge of trees, Ezekiel said as he prepared the story
for the child to eat. . . . An albatross flew into the wind & hovered there
as Sisdel hawed. Why was he laughing? We wish we could tell you.
Raisins & berries & red wine! The child could conceal her surprise no
more than her smile when mother goose swayed & the hen finally laid
its golden egg! We don't ask how, when, who, where, or even why —
because you understand, these questions no longer concern us. Time
reaches out & touches Time. The child saw us too, though she had
never witnessed the sea in such abandon. As much as any life is
a myth, yours is found in the father's image, Ezekiel continued, no
longer distracted by the wind or its words. The angel pursued &
then spit, determined not to let the emotions show. . . . Apples in the
morn, grapes on the vine. The father alas sensed this as his birth.
The monks now trading shirts as they crisscrossed the ridge, looking
down at the sea — the stork & crow circling back. Orpheus' father
hobbling toward the stone cliffs with us. The echo of a foghorn
coming somewhere from above the Aegean ruins & it was only then
that we looked out of our mediation & saw the girl playing with
Apollo in the fields. . . .

"*straw in the belfry,*" #47

—for sasha

You the one who lingers most, Ezekiel whistled to the bird as
a blue heron passed on his left side. . . . Ivy & mosquitoes & bye-bye
leaves, the bud of linden flirting with a curious light. The girl
coughed, nose running & the snot in her mouth. The man longed
most for the leaves' absence & in this too I understood him. . .
the honey & his own eaten prophesy. You make up our stories,
papa — do they hurt? she asked. A piece of straw in the toe & the
straw stalking the belfry tonight! Here, we have survived another
night. A hunchback's age & already witnessing violent trees &
winter's black wanting. . . . The sacrifice when it saw the eye's lament &
afterwards saved the world. *O love's self no longer real & it's not
loneliness.* A cobblestone ritual, the temple's pain where the
poplars converge in the shape of a horseshoe. *Beauty so rare. . .* &
miraculous, where do the figures go today? The earth skulls
changing through the leaves & oddly, this too a muse she recognized.
Like this, papa? she asks, making the forgiveness appear. I could cry
while telling you this, but at the moment in bloom, the trees turn left
& enter the monastery alongside them. We watch the sky foretell
another passage. And when we look at the most simple hill, our eyes
awaken. . . . The skin motionless, donkey ears listening, even
Orpheus wanting all of the distance. An original face counting days
says bye-bye blackbird. Bye-bye, black sheep! I pick up the maple
leaves, a piper's son. A ghost falls from the heron's cry. The deaf monk
chanting well, and for no purpose. A hair of her head in our
mouths. . . .

"redemption & a first dream," #48

—for john high

On the hill she saw the sphinx open its wings. A sacral sky
with shrines & the dead covering thick shrubs & vines. An old man
walking back to the place. . . . What, what will the grasshopper say
today! As if ascending an utterence blossoms. Paradise on earth &
the river echoing as the spheres pass one another over rooftops &
the river echoing again. Then the days come, you take stock. A
figure arms raised & hailing as if. As if a papa & you're tuning your
voice the piper says staring at the plum not alone or misplaced in
these accidental leaves. Papa! The child sighs, churning with the
nursery rhyme. Nostalgia arrives & you see us picking berries.
A practice while the sky recedes & returns, and someday you will tell
us, Orpheus grins, trailing past the fern & birthing. The compassion
you want & hold & illusion of narrative when you began with the
spotted owl, there were others. The monks clucking & clinging to the
rooted trees. *Virgin as a lamp containing the light.* Redemption
blinded first dream you siberia delphi & snow in the mist of
gold-rimmed leaves. *Isle of poets let me board your rounded spoon!*
What is it you want us to catch? she asks. And is it a birth as
nothing but you & the vision remains. The child a woman the man a
piper the wind a sphinx hovering upwards! The cranes' whiteness &
yes then the horizon's crossed openings. Ezekiel & the goose way up
in the middle of the air! No one, no one has died here. No, no we
anwser. Still you have died three times in as many days, papa.
Sasha? Hum. The weather is haphazard & the days follow gophers &
owls & horrific wolves & these strong poppies & azaleas
in beauty. . . .

from CEREMONIES (1984)

*I believe that almost all our sadnesses are moments of tension
that we find paralyzing because we no longer hear our
surprised feelings living . . .*

*because we stand in the middle of a transition where we
cannot remain standing . . .*

*the future enters into us in this way in order to transform itself
in us long before it happens . . .*

*the future stands firm, dear Mr. Kappus, but we move in
infinite space.*

How should it not be difficult for us?

—R. M. Rilke, *Letters to a Young Poet*

---

from THE IMAGINARY SHEPHERD POEMS

How I Saw Her

Listen, Papa. Movement of stolen light. Her body sweating
in tall grass, jasmine. When I touched her sides I felt a

small earth in my hands, a hunger. The way her body
trembled like oak fire. Not quite that. She was the word
never. Never to swim her waters. Never to see the world
washed up inside.

   I wanted to die into her. Mud singing our bodies together—
a resonant indulgence suitable for fish, waves. I thought
I heard a voice in the water saying—with your dreams
scattering like nameless tombs, try and catch a breath.
Maybe not from the river, or her. The past reaching its hands.
The future retreating from the current of her eyes.

   I wanted milkweed, a scent of childhood. The dogs close
when me and Jesus slipped the fence and ran it all the
way. Swamp. Cottonmouth. Underbrush. She reminded me.
Dark shore of her shoulders like the muddy bank of
nowhere left to run. When she buckled her legs around my
waist, I just wanted to die there, let the wind carry our
shadows.

Papa

Today Papa, I am no longer concerned
with being a man.

I am no longer concerned
with this woman who takes leave
from my mouth,
sideways.

If my shoes don't fit correctly, well then Papa —
to hell with it.

Or if my legs are too short
chop them off

Papa, today I am in between something else
and dirty hands,

in between the barber
circling wildly within his blade
and the blood stained t-shirts off street boys.

I know that I am not here, Papa
that I never was here,
I know.

And if I could find that one behind me
the man with no eyes in his sockets,

the one with his wrists
always handcuffed

in a blue pocket —

that would be something to talk, about
wouldn't it, Papa?

Circular Edges

I have dreamed myself to sleep
trying to put aside the sound
of Christmas bells.

Their orchestration has caught me by surprise
at so many forkings,

it's hard to distinguish anymore.

The few others, friends past known to me
what if I called them,
brothers.

Jimmy, do you listen?

Together we coughed out the notes
below the ceremony,
covering the darkness of vacant rooms.

We almost made it
into an absence where the street's
decorated song

left a naked desire, drunk

and receding down another alleyway;
hustling a wind full of more than
our shadows.

We couldn't deny it.

We couldn't shake its namelessness,
the cold that stripped us,

almost found us
shapeless,

and eventually it had me tucking you in
beneath the manhood,

the snows that refused to leave
your body.

Even after that
by the year's turning
her circular edge began to reappear

as the ashes ground
and accumulating
outside temple light.

A washing away.

Like a tongue's leaf
spiraling toward nothingness,

I am momentarily winded into a sky's parting.

The Rain

Lately I've taken
to walking across the park
as an imaginary shepherd.

I'm captured by the absolute
of knowing nothing.

Last night, away from all the faces,
Jimmy, I'm never more alive than this.

It's a difficult story
how distinctly she discovers
her path back
inside me

where she points one way
and then to its opposite

as if I am to follow   the night
weave between these distant motions.

I'm amazed by her proximity
to an objectless air: the clear unbinding

of a world outside
color.

How she undoes the light's direction.

Initiation

Some mornings I awaken now
to the talk of priests gathering
by the roadside,

the crested bonfires
ascending along the fields.

These holy men pray with the final upheaval
as crows lift into dissolution,

and we are empty of it out here.

Out here we drown the waters
swelling toward our solitude.

Some men speak in knives,
some in rivers.

Occasionally, I even converse with the pilgrimages
moving into the hills,

the goats who come nearer each day.

38

Our bodies never touch now,
But for some reason she comes within me

through the normal evenings,

shedding opaque orbits
around her guarded world.

Though I am hesitant to go
and abandon a life that's grown into me,

this time, we are building a connection.

Last Night

a partisan
came into my room
as if he wanted to inquire
about the exit
as though that exit
was only a wind
into another place
and there are no more
doorways
just a cliff of dark
the air holds
at the edge
while someone stands pointing
the other way
leading to the garden
mulching downward the cornered patch
of its earth
where he is now thinking
how to forget the way through
disappear
beyond the opening back

After Water

Jimmy, where can I find you tonight
to breathe through your death,

the almost nightmares
you left me.

She said I was wrong about dying,
but once inside her

I could see my separate lives
decaying into a ritualistic walk

ancient as the culture you saw
grinding itself down.

With time I became obsessed to uncover
the passage that sculpted into her
a delicate formation,

pure as a revolution's fiction,
yet enveloped in its anatomy.

Starving perhaps, unaware of hunger,
but among those you and I traveled

there was only a dissipating silence.

Most of us never left our birth,
but we heard different voices —
like when you said,
the trading of lives is blue
given to tribal response.

Was that your voice
exuding a color like blood

as in a fog each night of our youth
we arrived on the street corners
alive, yet ghosted.

We turned our backs on everything
but death.

The Partisan

this is not the hour I came from
but I return here after
the nameless depart me
breaking away
the spoken air
until they call it all together again
burnt leaves gather their shrines
at the hill's bottom

the morning reaches back to them
voices their own
white dreams that burn me
into a different waking
and I Fall out   hearing them
is a home I don't circle back to
before black pines in a separate hour
carry down these edges
a pair of cold hands
and I touch underneath
their waters'
primordial light

If Sleep

Father I have been standing
six days, and nothing has happened.

It is as if I never become here.

I smoke, disregard the tourists,
occasionally wipe the stains from my sides.

Suddenly I'm in the museum again
where as children
we speak in tongues concerning the dead,

and I remember you like the St. Thomas
we don't visit anymore.

Only I begin with his prayer,
the moon, the old brother stepping out
to dance in it.

The stars go up on the sabbath,
and still nothing happens.

Others arriving after us.
Even the beggars in uniform.

This time we don't wear them.

She is silent as a cathedral,

its hushed meditation.

Order resonates about the heart
in usual function.

The story continues
without me.

I am bleached abysmal
and blue.

But we are in this together.
Once more she is collecting
the self's pieces.

Her image now watches me
from her park.

Blue Hand

The stars won't look at me tonight. I know they have
seen through me. I pace the kitchen floor kicking
trash aside. A mouse scampers beneath my feet. I reach
down to touch his white, but he is gone. Mama crying
alone in an abandoned doll house. I don't know
where we go from here. I see this ragged man outside
my window every night. He lifts his head from a
manhole. Why he doesn't climb out, why I leave
wounds on the floors, I don't know.

Sometimes we forget ourselves. I dream of a hooded
man hanging from the moon's waist. Other times I
feel the law of another close around my wrist, a rough
blue hand rushing below the earth.

Washing

Jimmy, where something might be sacred,
I've grown sick.

Where my own violent
stripping begins,

and a vacuum like blue skies
enters,

I am without definition.

My meshed identities
no more than a rag-sewn ball

aimlessly rolling in a sphere of musics
not my own.

She shed my amorphous stories
to go ellipsing around each blind description

I give the world.

I can't touch them anymore.

Where is your death?

Apparitions

Papa, you've shaped the years of my life
into a burning.

Well, sometimes — even without her
this lake, the waters
near your plot

excuse my expectations,
the random forms I try to give them.

My seeing not contained
in said measurement,

in all the distance we carry with us.

What if I awoke one morning in pitch black
and went out into that storm.

What if there are angles
unknown to the eye's initiation.

They traverse us,

and this evening I drop their tuned
obituaries

into a music pure as fluid
channeling the main arteries,

like the child who looked back
one winter

as if seeing an untold God.

What if it takes a long while
to cross the threshold

through the almost hymns, the nameless calling.

For a moment, obstacles distill.
This world quiet as the subtle tones
of those planted beneath me

growing without a response,
this psalm.

Departure

for Lori

Everything still.
The quiet after —
    the rain is finished now:
the sound of no need
to bother. But night arrives
again, like it always does
as if to say
distance is never alone.
Only we misplace the words,
think of our hunger like another
desire; like our body embracing
new sleep,
yet knowingly   (in spite of itself?)
refusing all along.

What can anyone say.
Go on.
It never leaves you.
The blood is returning more than
what speaks out of silence,
completion.
The chestnut root sings, yes.
Blue rain on the window reminds you
of everything. Go on.
Open it.
This is the beginning.

Ceremonies

"The absence of God is his most complete presence." — Simone Weil

The water opens. I hear my life, its motion, a movement
beneath the motion. A white pelican stands at the
edge of surf, watches. He waits, then lifts with a rise
of sea and drifts on. At one time I thought myself a
kind of wind.

Some days it's easy. An Irish setter chases sandpipers he
won't catch. The sport of it, and we want more. In
the waves there are faces. They look out of the water
no longer afraid, in dance, in constant turning. They
remind me. We rise, but return. The fisherman here
looks at no one, and still, he is not in a dream.

After sitting at the lake all night my fathers could come
home with nothing. When I return I find them sleep-
ing by the bones of cow. Their lives over now, and
nothing. But fish were usually on the table, sometimes
perch. Not a small blessing.

The days I see I am wasting my life there is only one
moment. It holds me still, as after falling one re-
mains still. It passes. We make do. But all the hands
that cross over the plate. I wanted to grab one, violently
shake it—as if I could coerce the dying, find weight
there. They take me to Rilke: a boy slight, studious and
frightened. How he later wrote from a tower, snowed

and listening. A quiet man walking through the
whiteness.

Another blue gull eases to shore. Her wings flap the
wind. A flock of them gather across the bank of sand
like pharaohs. Once I woke to find the bird dead,
lying beside my pillow. The cry. Old song. We forget
so much. I think if I could leave my feet I would
understand this is not mine—the ground I walk, prints
of sand, the praise of some other.

The fog horn sounds off in the voice of a man calling. It
brought me here. It lets out light warnings when all
is clear. A music to that with an absence of notation.
This matters. I realize I want that song. Orpheus sing-
ing, not listening. To move the years inside a water
no longer our own names.

The fisherman tilts the cap over his eyes, pulls in the
albacore. It's over for now. The slow walk home,
beyond wind. That's why he comes here. He could take
a stretch of water in his hands and hold it for days,
waiting.

from THE LIVES OF THOMAS:
EPISODES & PRAYERS (1991)

in the day when you devoured the dead you made it alive.

"When you come into the light, what will you do?"

do you hear us still? in this day of our mutual birth and dying?

"When you make the two one and when you make the inner as the outer
so that the male will not be male and the female not female
then you shall enter. . . ."

—The Gospel According to Thomas

from TRACKS

---

image

finney tracing maps of the nile&
red sea from old national geographies.

55

(1951.) that kind of ease. the drawer full
of them within an hour. how imagination
tricksters. his daddy the preacher believing
the pharisees stole the sacred scrolls from the
river, carting them off to the dead sea when
his mississippi was so much more alive. hep
man. hep man thomas they called him. daddy to them
all. crocodile king. the faint lines blackening around
the edge of a folded page. finney's worlds taking
shape. catfish in the waters. all the fragments.
then a half-cracked bowl. the gold
fish flickering across the maps as the waters
pour forth& go lost, a treasure in his field without
knowing it. finney almost empty as the pencil is
laid on the table. accomplished in these beginnings.

a movement& a rest

the bad ju ju is what the eye wants
our old lives no longer
requiring attention. they possess
so many fields
—have you discovered the beginning so that
you inquire about the end?
not that their love
the cha cha midnight of quiet
evenings is over (us)
—you make eyes in the place of an eye then?
charlie hypnotized by a slight hum
change the dial on the radio he says
no more of that nashville shit
finney doubled in language by this repose
that loves us for no reason
at all
darkness inside of darkness
the many who are first will become last
you made it alive
pissing up& down this road

hitchhikers

P.S. Charlie, don't lie.

I. *the highway*

    November already. Charlie, I mostly picture her when
I think of last Christmas, on the road together—that map of
the world she handed over while standing on the corner of
Burn&Maple, scratching her thighs like a miniature cat and
that was somewhere south of Toledo. The partially gutted-out
hotel off Route 90, *The Bosie Hex* it was called, where we
opened pawn store gifts. The thick shades she bought me in
the dead of winter and the pair of blue alligator high heels I
swore we stole her while gigging my way through Florida& (I
never been to Florida and she knew that, Charlie). We
bundled tight against the cold, fucking early, smoking brown
cigars no bigger than baby fingers, drinking cheap holiday
champagne and pretending to listen to the imaginary silence,
the scarred hobo hooting& cat calls& the neon flicker of the
drugstore mall. Fingering my sax she had me scoot it between
her legs hawking a Parker tune all dizzy and later she called
home to her sister but she don't have a sister Charlie and you
know that& we didn't have the vaguest as to how to approach
it. Those mornings she woke kissing me all over, that perfect
o-ring sexy mouth, as if it were she who breathed out the
almost warm January winds that came with us across the great
plains. I can honestly say she was thankful, Charlie. Even
appreciative I'd returned from Ohio& left you for whatever—

58

choose your luck, so drunk I'd never believe anything you said,
spitting out *duck their kicks& still crawl up their legs* as if it
meant something? Appreciative I'd come back, yes, stealing
her away from those moonshine suckers, your daddy& what
he'd do& hell no I felt no remorse not for you or him or
anyone, why should I? It was just a boot-leg on the ridge, the
old man& we can't figure you out either Charlie, so fuck it.

II. *catwalking*

Shit, her dancing by the side of the road.
By the time we got to Montana
winter ferns& cactus blooming out of season,
then that sudden Denver snow
crossing the Rockies.
All those white storms followed us
through the mountains
'til we made Seattle& the north woods.

her fine contours/
apparitions really
against the stage shadows/crawling
shooting beer joints& strip
halls for a few bucks
a shit palace to sleep
in

Tooting God   this is change
if you look hard enough.
Nothing like your meanness&

fear of everything out there, Charlie.
No. Go on& die. We shined it—

goosing love& forking all possible roads
born that way since no backsliding's
allowed& (I reminded her every damn day
no turning back)
we killed your daddy.

dear charlie,

no we didn't like those other men lumberjacks mostly eyeing
her down whistling dixie big tease snapping peep hole show
beats& my jazz like it was real our own but you know katie
always did have her own mind not to be obliging or about to
owe me& ah yes you were right charlie& no i couldn't talk her
out of nothing& yes it was her money& her body& yes you
were always right about one thing charlie i'm a fool wanted to
make it on my own& yes for both of us& yes maybe even to
come back for your drunk ass once the cash started rolling&
we set things right got a home& a place because you're still our
brother no matter& jesus did i believe jesus learning it all over
now starting from go you hear me charlie you hear me mo'
charlie you hear me

III. *landscapeshoes*
            (*ghosted*)

Down the coast
we hopped freight, laughed& joked for three weeks
dreaming up fantasies about California.
Jumped the tracks in Novato
and damn near walked twenty miles.
We figured to shake famous
if not rich by summer.
Then we knew I'd have her love.
San Francisco, the foggy beach wine nights
talk bang sugar touching strange bodies
running whores& back table dice&
my horn like a little juju
man in gold before me
leading on/shuffling/rolling
rifts with the waves& top that man
(just you top it).
Coon shit asssassins/hundred
dollar hits/shimmied skirts&
the blind boys were all there
every night   making me think of her
black panties on the sand.
We'd kneel in the ocean
(hell, me scared of sharks)
you should have knelt down dammit!
Water washing around our waists/our sex&
practically froze my ass lots of times—
&sure Katie had her other boys
shotgun lovers she says
so I did the same.

Seemed so easy& dying&
mirage in the window watching
her with someone (was it you Charlie)
until she decided for herself—
I was either too much of men
or not one at all.
Until she finally took jealous
like we had for almost six crazy years
seeing her other brothers, her daddy, even
you on the mattress around back
where I buried him, Charlie—
buried him that son of a bitch.
Maybe we pushed things too far
but I just watched her walk away
sun sparkling on those blue
alligator shoes.

IV. *multiple lives*

We read stories about all those fuckers jumping off the bridge.
They don't even sing. Bird boys. Flying. Claw voiced. Not me.
But three months gone now like the whole year will pass
regardless of whether she comes back. Each afternoon living
on its own. I sit here, a sliced pear lying on the magnolia desk,
that painted over mahogany dresser the two of us
discovered in Chinatown. Mornings we worked it smooth
Charlie, better than any music even—searched the pattern,
stripped it down. Staring out on those gray dusty hills/not like
home boy. Smell that lingering orange fragrance/just salt air,
sun& rain, but beautiful. Why can't we accept that?

I know one thing. It's memory that waits us, sure as the Blue Heel I bought her, and that rotting piece of saxophone brass leaning against the chair. Funny how I don't even want to pick it up anymore. Watching a glare off the waves skim its way across the blurred horizon. Blurred or blind myself, we can't tell. Alone mostly, that's the main thing. Who can instruct us better?

This is the story inside the story. Regardless of how I tell it. It doesn't belong to us. Anymore than you do. After all that fishing. Telling the truth?

V. *the end or*
(*your sister lied too, Charlie*)

Take imagination for example.

So what if nothing survives we say. Like you couldn't feel a knife if someone were to stab you. Pain that was not yet the · pain of love. Katie shivers, looks at the fire, licks my shoulders. Our last night on the beach, me seduced by that other man? (Was it you, Charlie?) I played A *Train*, later Monk, sure of that. How baby hovered over my throat, talking about you, waving that knife in my face, naked herself—telling us you were already dead& later on masturbating as she calmly talked from the water. See Charlie, this is what I think. The man I was that night didn't trust death, sensed it coming but couldn't face it anymore than we could admit to never really killing her

daddy or fuckin' anybody, chicken shit-faced but leaving you
up there to die alone& so I got spooked, bet your ass, couldn't
even play my own tunes& acting as if a lover, any lover could
uncover in the sand something violent enough to interlock
time—*make things connect you know* like notes all blending
together, like our music, the way everything fell from her
mouth in that moment.

Love we mean.

Love was six years of her hand always slipping between past&
present or two bodies pitched into a kind of endless solitude
together only those were her bodies& you were in one of
them& we were just the past approaching dream Charlie,
that's all.

The three of us lingered awhile
studied this handsome figure
just swimming the waves, sandpipers&
fish eyes turning on the surf's edge&
then the pigeons& that mysterious swimmer&
bopping in the water as she scopes me, saying
hush, it's ok—you got dreams as big
as the darkness, don't you?
Sure I answer.
Sure we do.
Did she really talk that way, Charlie?
(Did we?)
A complete black, moontide
water shy then crashing.
A faint cry lifting from a small mouth.

Did we know what she was saying?
Could I understand her, or us, or any of this shit
even now?

Have you seen her, Charlie? Come on, tell us this time, who
chose this face?

off route 90

the weeks begin slowly for them now. as if
in anticipation. or without any. she's forgotten
how to live, finding each turn for the image
a blind intersection, a crossing for the past that
can't be fixed into being. thus finney's other
fiction. what they do after hours designated
by habit. the blue air separating us. intention
left alone for a moment. a night presenting
itself as the matter of factness in a lamp.
a half empty beer. a bed waiting on its own
only. &just that.

she can't dream what will become clear, the
plot suspended when what they say is simply
survive. continue. a fine voice at times. sometimes
we know love between the acts of recognition. or
the personal as you say it. where they go after
work. sodom. gomorrah. new york. memphis.
all dead names. signals. yet possibility is
it all happening tonight as she prepares the clean
pillows, waiting.

playing tongues on new year's eve

tower of nimrods' origin in this tongue, our noah, flesh
of fish, moses on the bridge signaling us toward the waters,
do you remember, charlie—how they found you& finney
in a fishtrap on new year's morning—remember
our bodies covered in octopus, weeds, bass, some perch, then
the small shark you mistook as a mother as your real daddy
thomas in the shape of jesus the fisher waved us on? in the day
when you devoured the dead, you made it alive, when you come
into the light what will you do? do you hear us still? on this day
of our mutual birth& dying? on the day when you were one you
became two but when you have become two what will you do?
where to uncover the parched leaves, skins beyond the word
known to all tongues? tell us now in order to leave this, the other
fiction where we became them, can you hear us now? this the last
call, our only eyes, a final horn

image

maybe they come out of this longing for an earlier
language, one still flying toward absence when in
the story the eye takes its own& leaves us. or the mixed
whatever dice tumbling, a go at the cards& then there's so
little patience for politics in the world and why not? you're
tearing the limbs away from an animal small, too delicate,
refined, a part of the loving& it doesn't grieve itself
freely. common roads on the map that lead to more
roads? ok. i admit the idiocy, take every side of it like an
unexpected plane, a slow walk, the dissuasion
katie talked about. anyway, we give into
you as you give unto others and somewhere in the
bush is the bush perhaps = the changing frames of
time that once climbed.

the kingdom of the father is spread upon the earth
&man does not see it

the lizard's blooded river (tracks) pouring into

a field of movement at the edge

if this is all that's learned

then take it

from EATING THE VOICES

———

along her thighs

katie is the story& past anatomy

our contained desire/
the uncooked flesh

        a single one
        this darker language

        pieces of menstrual blood
        spotted along the banks

make it alive she says

        entering the
        kingdom of the ear

        trouserflies, detective potboilers
        telling your plots

—clues?

walking along the populations
that scatter before us

        watch for the world

------

wichita state psych ward

Sometimes I get so desperate for love I run down the street
with my cock in my hand. Look out over the buses to see if she's
there. Stare down all the shiny black cars like a coal miner just up
for the light. Crazy when the longing comes, quiet, late in the
evening—alone between the sheets. No automobiles. I spot the
moon's blood& think of home, the old temple, the Jesus freaks
running speed in the woods. The city sounds hold tight blue blood
sleep, terrifying like the empty tin cup on my pillow. Where are
you Charlie. Come back you can't die. *Shit on you preacher. You
don't know love.* The way baby squeezed me hard, waist first, then
thighs, down the deformed marks on my neck where she burned
me drifting that deep reach into her god domain. I burn
everything& it ain't what counts. Reach for the lamp but it s no
use. No one's there. Cry her name over& over again. Jacking-off
'til nothing's left of the skin. Smoking heroin like the rich boy
art-fucks at Fat's Bar, sipping bad-ass Jim Beam. Bang it against
the wall& fuck you too doctor. Mornings I eat eggs& try to forget,
writing bastard ballads about the dead, seeing her face all jazzed
up, drinking coca-cola, smoke in hand, leaning off the edge of the
bed, nothing but the smell of her thin muscles smothering my
face, her fish-white back better than no drug, no fuckin' rock&
roll jazz blues club numbers shit game mister. I burn everything&
it ain't what counts. Burn your god damn house down if you touch
her. Her nakedness, a smell of panties lingers in my clothes. I walk
to work everyday trying to wear it out, shake it down, horny—but

not as loud as the rooster the boys keep in the junkyard out back. I could cut his balls off every time he starts fucking—just out of envy. Just like Katie did when I refused her. Just like you Charlie.

solitary ones

       At just the right intersection there is no face, only
his body, drifting forward. Floating almost, somewhat
contorted—toward the table where Charlie's last letter sits by
the ashtray, causing him to think of a chopped off ear in the
shadows of the early morning. A chopped off ear? His own
perhaps, at least that's the way it strikes Finney as he kneels on
the floor, trying to remember how he got here. Who chose this
face for me he asks. As if for the last time? The only thing he
can remember now is Scooter Johnson's boys throwing him
against the wall, slicing away his ear, taking the little money
left and tossing his things out the backdoor, threatening to cut
off his faggot balls next time. Scooter's boys carried away his
horn& guitar. Because there are secret words& whoever finds
their explanation will not taste death.

       Finney rises to the table eyes darkened, elbows
trembling, peering over the envelope& broken bottles, trying
to find his way back from where the beginning is. Come on
Finney you can do it. This old terrain. Tucked deep in his
bruised skin. Finney sees himself in the other worlds for a
moment, blowing sax, dreaming this. He wants to pick up
Charlie's letter, shake out the words like the missing ear.
Caress the lobes, shuck the words& bones out the kitchen
window where all of his clothes& books lie in piles by the
garbage. The dead mouths. Where ears stand waiting. But he
can't understand his life, where the stories are leading him.

      Charlie's letter begins—brother, lover, mistress?
When you take off your shame no one puts it under a bush.

Taking no thought from morning until evening& from
evening until morning for what he puts on, Finney says, you
retarded mother fucker. Yet hearing the voice, the body re-
members itself. I don't want you here, get out of my life,
Charlie. Go on& fuck yourself on bad flesh& junk—daily
news from the massage parlor sluts who'll never love you.
Finney thinks of the man turned woman as he circles the
kitchen, the one he left lying in a northern river to drown like
his own old man. Thinks of the lover he grew up with&
believed in, the one who tried to kill him one night because
Finney couldn't accept the confusion of merged bodies.

He looks through the broken glass of the kitchen
window, touches the cuts left on his face earlier by Scooter's
boys, fondles the old burns sister Katie gave to his throat.
Finney knows Charlie's dead, this one he never wanted except
inside him like his own blood or the beginnings& he thinks of
the nights he slept on Charlie's shoulder afraid of everything
that moved, afraid of his own sleep& how Charlie could calm
him then, saying my mouth will not be capable.

Finney prays nothing to the old brother, the moon he
troubled under, the plot he's been born into—unaware of his
own face, the throat, the burns, his only physical memory of
voice. He walks past the table to the refrigerator, opens the
morning prescription. Whoever has ears to hear let him hear.
Say what, Charlie? He catches himself. Looks at the maps of
the Dead Sea plastered to the cabinet walls, his own mountain.
Calmly sucks down the handful of reds& bennies he's awak-
ened to every day for the past month. Empties the glass of
milk, takes an extra handful today, stares at the eyes from the
crucifixion that stare back from the living room wall. A first

74

smoke and the Albuquerque Tribune on this day he decides to die. The day he becomes Thomas. Starts the naming that leads into.

Finney blowing shit-faced in a Memphis bar the first night we found him. Just one of the readings. This son of a half-black preacher& a working man. A father who killed himself in the early evening summer heat on July 19, 1955, just in time for the boys& Katie to see the old Pentecostal daddy rolling into the river, huge-bodied, guitar like a vest clung to his chest, singing the kingdom of the father, he draws the sword in his house, sticks it in the wall to know if his hand will carry through, then slays the powerful fuck... Later the boys would make up lies about what they saw, inventing something new every time, never really sure if what they saw was Finney's daddy or not, Thomas the Doubting Disciple or a devil or an incarnation of their past. Perhaps just another ghost, already drowned in the body because it was so big, over 7 feet tall, unable to contain itself. Finney picks up the old man's notebooks he's saved all these years, images him once more. The desire that flowed into this face, the face he almost feels now, into the embraces that surprised even Katie.

He slides the envelope off the table, reads the return address, wonders about Charlie's funeral& whether attending the services could ever be the last horn. Wonders if Katie will be there. This is how it ends or begins, the story& its telling— the imagined as well as the real, where the two intersect& what we remember of it all anyway. That part of me that was him, the part of him that was us, filling in the rest because the telling is what's left = the anatomy of these blind tongues almosting it& drinking from a scorched mouth.

what hep man thomas told finney& bo the night he drowned in snake river

what's wrong with the world is people ain't got enough
money& the ones that do don't know how to spend it right&
if somebody starts singing good anyway cityfolks try to buy it&
if the music brings a hard price we lose another singer like
those little children who have installed themselves in a field
which is not the theirs& if you think there are enough good
singers it's like a mustard-seed smaller than all seeds so just
take a good look around or come stumbling down this river say
any friday night where there used to be plenty of us gathering
and hardly no radios or take my buddies for example sitting in
a barn that's only got more whiskey than lies yet when you
make the two one and when you make the inner as the outer
so that the male will not be male and the female not female or
when you make eyes in the place of an eye& a hand in the
place of a hand& a foot in the place of a foot then you shall
enter but they're still talking about who they could have been
playing with those nashville records so you can just walk
yourself down to town where everybody's dressed up
pretending to be somebody else's clothes while the outer& the
inner& the above is below us and when you make the male
and the female into a single—well you see there's just strangers
like you& me picking by ourselves trying to figure this river
out

he chose the large fish without regret

Trying to understand it like this, Finney. Reserved yet about
to yield. More often than not a memory& incarnation no better
than the lives creating them. A mustard seed. Three blind mice.
How often this doesn't matter anymore. Always forgiven but we piss
on forgiveness& this genuinely bothers me. Horsepiss. Sour wine. A
lot of evenings nothing but banjo tunes. Fine. A blackened cart laid
along her thighs. Clogging over this plowed soil& occasional hymns.
These kin eating the dried loaves of bread, their secret bodies. I
know for a fact God's holding nothing against us. Told me so. Like
when the hoeing's done& you can fall in the hard rows of tomatoes,
potatoes& peas. Reclaiming the love not past but constantly born in
our mouths. Sometimes it don't bother to hurt. We tell ourselves
this over& over—you shall enter. Lost in the waters. God is love&
loves all things the other Thomas, your Aquinas, said. Remember
Finney. The fishtrap on New Year's Eve. You're no baby no more
but you know my lives. Nights I held my own, listening as if a part of
the sounds. Shout a few flying rifts as they pass. The way the river
does becoming a single one. Or hearing it from the porch& drinking
black wine by the tracks you once rode to Ohio. All those years.
Troubled ain't the word for it. Misguided& admitted my wrong.
Considering myself a mouth, a preacher, a giver of words. Still him,
crocodile king& true Thomas all along. Mostly trying to expose
these fears so I couldn't hide them from myself. Telling your stories
in the garden of the rot. A pure fool either way. Who chose these
eyes for us you ask? Scrambling for love on the tracks, along back

alleys, pool halls, hardly existing night clubs. Bedrooms of friends&
their wives& let me tell you the taste of shame. It was leaving that
saved this mouth. No more turn aside& brood? Hearing you cry on a
boxcar. I still dream of all that walking home drunk& the others can
tell you I was good at it.

Crickets make better song still we live a ways from where they
teach you to do things pretty. My 12th rib gone. Among the fanshoal
of fishes. The sacrifice. One of the boys always boasting about last
year's rain among the living. Miss it? Or the someone. On the
spoons. No longer choking on the angeled songs. A man drowned.
Music hooted as if from the face of an owl. Clicking tongues on a
Jew's harp. Slapping against the wheelbarrow to catch the ringing of
horns. Evening will find itself with or without you, Finney. Horning
it. A hint of mandolin gets the old man cupping his hands around a
churchbell like a wine sucker juicing blues God only knows how.
Ghostwoman in the cupboard. You know me, Finney? Release it to
our fields then. Bet a dime no fool is whistling before we get a
chance. The one who came before you. Why? How the stars that
surround our field remind me of love if I'm in a good mood. Why
not? Why do you ask?

All vanished since? Look around. I don't know what to tell
you. These hands, their mouth, whose movements. Taste death. Fat
legged corn brush one another chattering like palms over a
washboard. A light breeze. Watch for the world. Dance better when
the owners come, boy. Even a scarecrow's legs kick to a bunch of
strong laughs. Empty you in& out of the world, Finney. Fires grow
across the roads. Pour out of their mouths. At ease with a life in a
straight cool air cooing summer night. Can't tell you origins. Only
that it won't come by expectation. I saw a face only once but in more
ways than one. Drum. I had no idea I was going to be your daddy.

78

Darkness in darkness remember hands& their source. You know how hard it is for you Finneys to talk about love. You were just beside us one morning. Then all of these musicians came stepping out of their barns = time came over here, clean-shaven, ready—maybe whiskeyed up, staggering as if still in dream& there was nothing to it.
Nothing to it.

lament

sand sifting sideways without the movement of feet

when the morning begins we find

our first thirst

sliver fish you set forth on the chopping block

an older thomas out there

the way he preached to the river

a rowboat leaning against the dock

the split oars

an absolute calm

blue water, black sky

ritual of the eaten

from KINGDOM OF THE ELECT

----

mustard seeds in her field

the difference between those
coming&
those going
requires a look at the hands
alive in the world
the dog barks when one comes or goes
if a response is necessary
go to the bone
smell our blood
what is appearance
&absence combined
finds itself here
among the corpses

. . .

an open mouth
knows what is enough
look inside
the blind speaking
a possibility of
speaking   the body's fields
stripped
&calling in this ridge of hills

alone   look again
sacrifice of the stoned pavillion
listen for
the eye's flicker& these sheep
gathering outside the rain
expansive steppes   shallowness of the stream
              &then
sun& stars&
romance you want to touch
what strikes within   the interior
of the nose's hair/   breath& impulse
when anyone comes or goes

. . .

what we see is not at this garden's edge
black ants crawling
about the sleeve
into your socks
somewhere we possess
a nowhere
whose God& love present
can't say it
a troubled affair&
without language as the mirage enters
to live in the deer as she runs toward
the hunter's call
our drunkenness&
crossing between the crushed stones
dusted heaps of gone grasslands
though death
begins
past their fields

. . .

these are the unspoken details
born out of so many days
walking
the vanishing skies& what follows
as the rains close in
thomas, why have you come so far
to hear so little
only the drowned
fish remain
in the waters do we
find such articulate difference
nothing comparable to emotion
because we know that outside it
we have no being

. . .

the
world   bends
the curtains
&converses the mirror
along the tracks
maybe her corpse
sustaining because
in this way
there is no shit beyond us
the test we set for them
they have passed

what country have they come from
find a moment
&smoke in it
if this is
all we have
celebrate the hour

of saying who you are like

the way finney rolled over& awoke in a different body.
thinking about time& how it loses itself in the blind mouths.
the changes& shifts of dream that go unnoticed in gesture.
pictures of you by the river we've seen over& over. this story,
the one already known& outside memory. we find ourselves in
it long enough to pick out the broken glass, glance to the left,
watch the phrase the worlds have long imagined. all gone
where? vertical air, parching heat, decay. he who walked the
waves alreadying& empty. yet you finneys gather some things.

finney intermittently swept up in this boat. the cargo carries
rot oranges, tangerines, gnawed walnuts. cliffs obliterated in a
blue heat. black steamers in the northern lights& these naked
boys swimming on the shore. absence in the plot causes them
to think of themselves, how the images continue, wilderness
moan by these deserted continents, who we've become
traveling the questionable identities. open eyes, dry stones,
flower of an unseen color. charlie striking a match to a small
kerosene light warming the hands, a single piece of bread. his
hope to survive the river goes on here. ghostwoman. ashes on
her breath. sand& stone& shells, what remains of the open
palms.

the earlier one so much opposed to morning light, his eyes
trailing across the water. dripping of the faucet as you sit on
the stool drying those hands. porcupines& squirrels in the
meadow. as the dead come about the love each drum plays.
looking at you from such deep graves, he'd rather do it like this
if necessary. solitude of cold afternoons. shared tea. the bodies
joining further in the unclosed fields. under the hills a forward
whiteness. scored light as music& the windows out into this
cleared darkness. bushweed& roof tops conducted along the
sloped horizon, a lone owl becoming the single one.

always this falling off to sleep in the middle. not a regret& not
a dreaming. the old thomas who sat beside us on the bed.
fish& seaweed smell mapping the sand. unrealized source. all
of the othering. each action arises by itself. 12 apostles having
preached to all the gentiles. worlds without end. their
fascination with knives connecting in loneliness for all that
comes. or pure destruction. form of forms which darkness could
not comprehend as memory unfolded it. of saying who you are
like, taste of death. the slow rite. bo donning his cap, dancing
by the blues guitar. saxophones horning the secret air, hidden
rivers, deep song of violent hands as ants cover us over& over.
warned against the complaining, celebrate the hour. play
it right then. walking finney from late evening to early
dawn& can we ever know this. the path obliterates
each bitter mystery.

tourists playing tennis in tan shorts across the beach. katie
drinking heineken this the first of every morning, black spots
in front of a blue sea. see it now. so distinct they're hardly
visible anymore. an image like vacations when she cuts the
stones. fearing jellyfish, all that can be witnessed in shallow
water. sailboats, even her distance narrowed. because disaster
is easier, predictable. seaweed floating to the beach. she combs
her hair. the body pretends. but this is only one face.
blackwater riverish again& forever in the brewing katie. now
we understand. sit calmly. wait. she looks into the reflection
the others gave her. partakes in every prayer staring back. so
much a fire in the ending. every century. her mouth is capable.
silver fish she set forth on the chopping block. singing.
&merging with the scenery. too quiet for her own liking some
mornings yet without resistance, perhaps. no longer desperate
in the troubles found. worship the time remaining, rain in it.
the slow growth& rain (reign) of rite.

mystery for waters. catfish& perch. cool wind eating the
beginning without end. drives them crazy when we forgive
ourselves, standing by the story. the characters incomplete&
washing hands. the new tunes no different, say finney. thicket
of brush, exposed sunset. maybe it's not the small shark charlie
witnessed in the net while running across the deck. just the
likeness of ourselves shedding near the edge of each false start.
fear left alone for a moment as you wanted to reach out for the

fin, the reefs pulling up again toward savage fields. others did it. other mouths. human shells, nearing it. this love, dry fog& the skins becoming fish.

communion of human bodies that precede them now. lining the shore you were sure of that. small cities disappearing past the hills. thomas in ghostshoes found drowned. sign of a white field. whose cultures? burrowing in. whose times? snakeskin. whose logics? determining each sequence? none now, whoever finds has no explanation. fanshoals, minnows, seaburns. the known word. morning moves itself in& without him. photograph of the worlds. carcass meat& hanging skulls. walk lightly we say. as if deciding the location for a picnic, for anything. blue air breath. foreign voices later& always pull awake dark songs coming up to meet them. strolling in a cotton shirt. meshed in the narrative that reminds each corpse. pieces of driftwood, octopus, shrimp, prompt repulse& scavenger blood, this price, what then? what the world wants when it finds itself. finney's repose. dismissed in the suddenness. ants gnawing each eye. so they will not be broken.

from THE DESIRE NOTEBOOKS (1999)

Selections from

The Book of Mistranslations
A Face of Desire
The Monks Overlooking The Story

PLACES OF

DESTRUCTION, FALLEN EMPIRES.

THESE ARE THE WORLDS IN WHICH WE

SHALL GATHER, THE BOY SAYS TO EZEKIEL AS THEY

STAND BY THE GATES OF THE OLD CITY. AND THIS IS HOW

WE SHALL KNOW ONE ANOTHER, THROUGHOUT TIME, KNOW THOSE

WITH WHOM WE BELONG

—*The Desire Notebooks*, 987
(original manuscript, Kiev)

when the centuries meet

What is it you're writing? the man inquires, rather too patiently as he pulls on her skirt and they stop before the stone bridge leading out of the city. . . .

Stagebrush shells, the obliterated brush and rot walnuts wasting in the fields. . . . she says, turning to him.
These letters are to you, she then whispers, folding the edges of the paper while pointing at the sun.

For a moment the man studies the curiosity of the onlookers faces.

She takes his tongue into her mouth.

This is what I've written—A way into the hour? And, there is a god in you too, but which god. . . .

There's your angel again. She laughs, turns the corner and walks further down the road.

The man's almost startled, but not quite. He stares at her gray hands, the angel standing on the sidewalk with burns covering his arms.

A blinded heap of bodies by the cliff.
Five monks walking to the sea.

Have you forgotten? she asks.

Turning the corner in the road now, he remembers. . . .
They sit, silent for an hour.
Under the hills a whiteness scored in light, one monk calls across
the road, waving a lantern, prepared to let the onlookers pass.

The west flank border patrols contained by this music too, these
surroundings. . . .

The sun's eye on the soldiers' uniforms. I remember all of the
armies that have come here, she says, pointing at the boys' faces,
their desire.

Though one day we'll see the large body of water called a sea in
the pages.

The sky will come down to us.

Skin-back hills. . . .
To do nothing takes courage? you will ask me, crossing the line
of death before we arrive.

He watches another woman by the tracks, selling carnations, singing–though he doesn't recognize the song.

On this day.

The angels will carry on with their business. Because you understand, treason can be arranged; love, hijacked.

The monk stands, lights the candle, touches the book, begins to walk across' the waters. . . .

The man's finding it difficult.

This is the country I write you from, she scribbles in the Notebook today, though it will be years before the man will read it.

He quietly strolls beside her now. He wants something. Perhaps to kiss her.

So that in this way, you will father his child! the monk calls out.

Our child. . . . Ezekiel says, skipping ahead in the story. This one they have come to believe in.

Who gives you the words?
Why don't you ask where I found the paper, Ezekiel says to Sisdel.
Look there are raspberries on our vines!
Tell mysteries to those worthy of mysteries? Mika asks.
The dead being buried in gardens today.
Why our need for repentance then? Virgil burps.
If divided we'll be filled with darkness, Hezhen caws.
There are human shells, older than our story, Sisdel insists.
All day the sun has remained behind the clouds, yes.
They're scattered about the road . . . these human shells, Hezhen again
hisses.
He hasn't translated the chapter that speaks of the child?
So naturally the man is timid as he watches her in this sky which
could again become a night.
Our birth into the world of men?
A moment of horizons, Sisdel.
Lean into your hips, your sex, your mouth, she smiles while
pointing at the sky. . . .

from Hezhen's journal

93

TOMORROW

Foremost, the brown soil, fences rolling into the hills, as
if backwards. That moment unlike any other, because I had begun
to sense my failure. Finally, after all of these years. In my death, it
would change. There are things I tell no one. For instance, my life
was never a story and could not become one. And imagine, I had
thought of black leaves, a burning bush, water no longer a part of
my sex. Everyone had gathered, our monks, the boy, Father—
though he, too, was almost completely blind. I began to see shad-
ows and pots. I looked at the white. Something in the air, cherry
blossoms, almost pure. Today when we say good-bye. She was
kinder this way, they will say. She was almost among us.

    The monks singing.
The boy waiting to escort you as he has those before us.

The First Morning

When he woke up that first morning without her on the road he was no longer surprised. Though he didn't know where he had fallen asleep, or how long he had been sleeping. The black crow flew up to the side of the one-eyed boy. The crow hovered there watching the movement of sable over the frozen water. The man sensed then that the boy might be an angel. He had read about the crow in her Notebooks. Where are you from? he asked the boy.

I came from the monastery east of these hills, the boy said, pointing with his scorched arm which was again burning. That is where her father actually died, not long after completing his work.

The black crow stared toward the hills also now.

Is that where we're going?

He could hear the trains passing over the tracks to the south, the call of their laughter, then the odd sound of ice cracking.

Someday we could go there, the boy said.

How did you get your burns, the man then inquired.

When I was like you I went out searching.

The boy stepped forward. His short-cropped hair red and uncombed, his left eye white, his good eye blue.

Would you like to go beyond the road, into the forest? he asked.

What will I find there?

A cross and a rose. More stories. A sacred book. Perhaps a storm at night. . . .

Questions.

The truth of why you have come here.

Well, go ahead then. Take me there.

You will have to come on your own, the boy warned. If you want to hear the story I have to tell you, you'll have to vanish on your own. Without her.

Thus they had begun their walking.

IN EZEKIEL'S GARDEN

A god in her, but which one? Mika the Blind asks as the ceremony commences in their garden.

The lovers outside the dream, casually smoking, Ezekiel says, stepping out of the pages, again pouring their green tea.

We came to watch as the couple walks about, Sisdel—the handless monk—tells the others, looking about the room for the one-eyed boy Thomas, who has again ventured out with the man.

Perhaps we have just been sleeping much longer ourselves, Virgil whispers into Ezekiel's ear, addressing him as 'Old wise one'. Perhaps that is why the lovers have again awakened our desires? Virgil says before breaking into hysterical laughter.

Just as in the Notebooks not only our lives, but their lives are revealed, Hezhen hisses.

Sisdel offers forth his cup. But how? he asks. In this hour of Sundays?

day eight

If there were time, she thought. The man looked at her face and tried to understand the changes. I really didn't believe the music, she said. The first time I heard it. This was her own music, he knew. The quality of the voice. Noble fir, Christmas lights, the face of another as she lay beside him now, trying to recall the balloons, a windmill, the ancient texts she had seen in the library as a child. If there was time, she thought.

Hand and nose, ears and neck. The coachman laughing as the ferry crossed the river. Her meditation on a desert. Because she knew. Go to the left, she told him. When you find my home. You'll find tomatoes, bananas, this moon. The history made blood. The sun will become an object.

Her hands trembling when he caressed her.

He denied it, but he knew.

The crisp blue marks on her throat, the cancer growing.

day eleven

. . . . Such a myth we want to tell. Surely you see. One full of wonder, conviction, belief even honesty if you will allow me to use this word? I have seen you in Constantinople, Rome, in Babylon. Your face written on the white pillow as your hands speak, moving through the dry air, this windless, winter afternoon. The way we tried to restore the love, mere travelers, having been given a train. along the river. This flock of black crows. See their faces squawking. The blue heron and white egret in the shallow? Everything returning to where I once began. This movement backward and forward in time. This is how I know you. The fresh track along the river which ceases to be a river because you don't yet see it. Here you are. Soon we will escort you there. To this haven where our voices take refuge, come in from the snow. I welcome your problem. Because once there was a river, and then there wasn't.

In the next dream her father had told him this.

BACK ON THE ROAD

The crow turned to him as they walked into the clearing
past the forest to their east. This is what I want to tell you, the
one-eyed boy said, now breaking the silence they'd walked in for
several days, hearing only the crunch of their footsteps on the ice,
the snap of branches falling in.

The three-foot, black crow nuzzled under the tip of the
boy's shoulder.

I want you to stop thinking love is so difficult, the boy
smirked, lighting another cigarette.

But I don't believe love is difficult.

You deceive yourself by saying otherwise, the boy snick-
ered. To do nothing takes courage. Do you understand? You your-
self have decided to come here. Sometimes to do nothing takes
courage.

The black crow flew into the snow, let out a deep, hor-
rific squawking.

How long do we continue walking, the man inquired.

How long can you stand it? the boy responded. Their
kingdom is tucked between the hills and the surrounding forest
on the other side of God's face.

Do you want to go there?

Since to travel, first of all, is to change one's body, the
crow said, as if mocking the sky.

DESIRE NOTEBOOKS

For just as the wounder wounds himself, the healer heals himself, Peter said to Ezekiel after falling from the sky and they began their stroll across the centuries, each wondering how to cure the other's pain.

Ezekiel searching for a way to part the waters, then deciding to simply walk across them.

—The Desire Notebooks, 989
(original manuscript, Kiev)

day seventeen

Whoever comes into my mind find& the beginning of a
story she had written in the notebook as a girl. And this is how
she had begun her life as well, as if writing her own future. An
excuse for living, she told the man today, standing by a snowed-
over corpse, rolling up her shirt-sleeve in the snow, pitting the
needle to the base of her wrist. That's what you want. An excuse
for living? Or finishing things in the present tense?

The man's acrimonious grin, his somewhat distant
expression this morning. All night drinking. No one understood.
Her passion. But then there had never been time to consider her
own feelings. Sometimes a face vividly becomes a story, he agreed.
One possessed with the mythic quality of touch, or smell. This is
what's most difficult for you, she went on as he spat, put out the
cigarette and pounded the road with his forehead, as if trying to
crush it to death.

The choice is yours.

ON THE THIRD NIGHT

When the boy stopped walking, and it was clear that
there was no more sky, the crow glanced momentarily to its left
where the man was leaning on his knees, panting, already wanting
to write his letter. Did you really love her the night you left, do
you think so? the boy asks.

Yes.

I wish I could love her.

Do you love her tonight?

Yes.

That's not true.

If you love her, why are you here with me?

The man comes to a full stance, stares himself at the blue
mountains partially glazed in ice, the lost roads, the boy with his
dirty face—the black crow and its red beak squawking at the
group of monks trudging over the hills to the stone walls of the
monastery. She's dead.

Yes, it's good that you actually say it.

What will I find, if I go there? the man asks, looking at
the blue mountains.

I can't tell you that. But its not what you expect, your
pain.

He hears the monks are singing as they walk—carrying
on about something or another in a chant too distant for him to
make out. The black robes against the white snow, the blue hills,
this absent sky. The one waving appears to be blind and his head
is shaved.

Yes, that's Mika, the one-eyed boy Thomas says. He's the
blind one.

Which story?

The one dreaming in the snow. Like the one you will write about in your letter to her. The one you have no confidence in, the boy grins, wiping some of the dirt from his chin.

He starts in after the boy, who has again started walking. But it was the crow that started walking first, as the monks on the hill retreated into the snow somewhere. Even the apostle Peter, the smallest of them all, as he joked with Ezekiel about their world's renewal in this destruction.

ON THE THIRD NIGHT

These bright colored skulls. On a postcard from child-
hood she had saved in order to remember her life. Or the place of
it. The monks' home. Over the hills, on the other side of God's
face, her father had told her as a girl. But his death was less an
issue of memory than revision. That bothered her. Oddly. O
father—where has my voice gone? Did she say this to him when
she last saw her father? There was his dream, and her dream to
come, but she didn't tell this man. Couldn't. She watches his facial
muscles, his motionless eyes, a mocking smile as the train takes
them further into the darkness. What did she really know about
him, or the self she had invented for him in order to reveal this
story? His advances, gestures, habits—his speech and dreams she
now recorded in the notebooks. A ghost or shadow, golden leaves,
an outdoor cafe by the pond. The face of her mother then. As if
she were charting a map of their world on this man's body. A post-
card she had mailed to herself in childhood from a garden district.
Her mother and father standing by a pond. She stuck it in his
pocket.
    She had written: My body is a map of their world.
    When he awoke, she showed him the scars to prove it.

NAMING THE STORIES

The one-eyed boy had turned to him after he left the last
village, signaled him further down the road. The man's feet were
tired, and he saw a yellow light coming up over the horizon.
Glazed white hills. Morning had found him and the boy togeth-
er. The angel awoke in his eyes as he approached the blue skies.
The boy's arms ashen, his small gray hands appearing tentative in
the yellowish light. A wolf in the clearing, waiting—as if to carry
him back to his own life. Do you have any more cigarettes, the
boy asked.

He tied his shoes, drew in the cold air, re-read the words
of his last letter before her death:

Dear You,
I'm afraid. Are you afraid tonight? Not of history that
is . . . not the wars . . . not even the stories. What does it mean to be sep-
arate while we walk together all day? See that darkness we sometimes
call night. Where is our house? What if once finished with it all, we
find it was as easy as saying something like—haven't I told you that
I love you?

day eighteen

The future held a peculiar significance for her afterwards. After kissing this man while he slept. Colors, smells, locale, perhaps tension in the weather. She remembers the boy laughing, crossing the hill to the monastery when she was still herself a girl—the first time she had seen her father's collection of letters. As if Father were shaping each name into a country, she told the man earlier, taking his hand, strolling up and back down the corridor of the train all day. A dead face she saw beside him in the corridor then, her mother's—though the memory of her mother's face had begun to fade long ago. . . . The boy had taken her hand too—though she didn't know how to explain this to the priest— led her to the lake where the monks were gathering walnuts and acorns. Something involving a conflict, yet she couldn't quite touch it and didn't know how her life would actually end now. Sticks and stones may break my bones, the monks had chanted jovially.

The boy later became an angel, but I and the boy had plotted out the distance to Lake Baikal together, she'd said, trying to describe it. . . .Walked there in the spring from the monastery. And the boy put his hands in the still frozen water. Fish. The eyes of the fish were different afterward and the boy then miraculously withdrew one of the fish from his mouth! A large sea bass unknown to the lake . . . and then I saw my mother's dead body float to the shore.

A child discovers life and death, an encounter with fish. Walking back to her father's room, the boy had informed her how he would die while drawing still more fish from his mouth.

The fish flew into the sky as white birds.

I will never forgive you if you die!

Forgiveness is perhaps the greatest thing we can do.

His eyes different that morning, the fish flying. . . .

But now, your eyes are different too, she told the man
when he awoke, though while you slept I entered your body as
you have entered mine.

day nineteen

You'll think of the hills sometimes, the purpose for leaving
that which was known to you. Fragments of memory weaved, the can-
dle in your bedroom, the monk's bed, which will be your bed—my
hands. . . . The way I touch you now. You'll come to see my hands, or
hear them, as a voice from which your own identities arise. A per-
sonal history, yet no one can tell you this—the pain in your groin, the
unkempt desire. Try to tell me why we die. Sporadic gunfire in the
hills. A shifting sense of time: you will also move on, as my father, as
the other Gnostics in the story. Blue and yellow, a leaf you hold tight.
On the trains with another one day, a remembrance of our day, this
page, this chronicle of your own life divided. Cleanly wipe your oak
table, take up the parchment. Hear their voices below. A squirrel runs
by, you see a deer in the field, your angel, a fox, a blue jay. You are
older, but you are almost like a woman. Call you a child, if you like,
promiscuous. Neck flush to a white collar. Reading the liturgies,
counting balloons. This household on the mountain, I love you. A
place in my mind This is why I write, forming an angle of triumph
for the piano I will no longer play—the candle, a chair, my spoiled
window looking out.

This was the first of her letters the man had translated.

THE NEXT DAY

Tell me, where is it you really want to go? the boy asks.
Do you want to carry the sky, or do you want the sky to carry us?

The three had finally reached the point on the hill where
the man had last seen the monks singing.

Your unhappiness, is it like this field? the boy then asks,
pointing to the cemetery beyond the fields of the monastery.

It's where I wake up, the man started to explain, but
thought better of it.

If it's where you wake up, where is it you sleep? the boy
asks, though these words again startled the man for they came
from the beak of the crow.

In my dreams?

No. In your sleep.

In my dreams. I can't say. There are so many faces.

But one is hers. Is that what frightens you?

The man stares over the wide breach of frozen ice toward
the lake and field and monastery before them.

Draw a face, the crow suggests.

The man takes hold of the boy's burnt wing and brings it
down to the snow, begins to map out the features he sees.

A moment later the crow stands back and studies the picture.

Yes, it's a peculiar face, the crow says, noting how much
the face resembles its own.

Yes, the boy agrees. Quite peculiar.

The two then begin to pee in the snow together, covering
the face.

Life damages people in the most simple ways. It is the
face of her child that you see. But there is something else. You

110

know her better. Can you remember the child now?

This is my dream?

Why do you think it's a dream! the one-eyed boy shouts.
He then sweeps away the remains of the face in the snow, and they
start walking on the lake, which later became a road, and later a
sky, and even later—a story. Though it would be much time
before the man would see it like this, and only then when he saw
it with her.

day twenty one

The ghost—its history rose of the stone—like the cob-
blestone bridge she had once crossed at the age of twelve. They
were talking about Jesus on the road, and she had started to fear
his presence. An outsider—choosing between place and jour-
ney—one of the monks had touched her on the shoulder then. As
if to acknowledge the bleached-out huts, the domed church of
worshipers—the Old Believers behind her. To travel, first of all, is
to change one's body, the monk instructed her. Why did she
remember this now? Designated hours for looking at her shoes.
Or a dialogue with the world she felt occurring whenever she
touched this man beside her on the train.

Tell us what we already know, she whispered.

The boy looked about.

Tell us the truth of what we already know.

A shadow falling on the door to the tracks.

day thirty four

A sound in the dark. She heard it this morning. That ebb
to her father's voice. It suddenly reminded her of someone she
used to be. Memory no longer of use. She thinks of a road map
without streets. Her father rising in pain. When I lived there. . . . she
says. Who knows why we talk of death. Don't tell me it isn't worth
the trouble, though. She sees the man's hand now. Trust me. I will
be there tomorrow. . . .When we depart the train. A draft in the
coupe.

This priest who pretends to be her father as she is dying.
But he cannot take away the pain.

When I was a child.

Passion before I was dead, she cried.

day thirty seven

Why this need to carry on? She had asked him the
next morning, not as a rebuttal but as if to get at the source of his
anguish. A watch, a stone, the silver tea cup he kept in his bag.
Your memory will begin to unfold in this way, many years later. A
sign by the tracks. The angels, you too have again seen them on
the road. . . . I wish I could understand, he said. No train had come
for two days, and now it was again approaching the time of depar-
ture. So the couple walked on.

To carry on? The closer I come to you, the more I forget
the details of my own life, she'd said, stumbling along the tracks
in the dawn light, rhetorically answering her own questions. As if
the voice of her father had been interrupted during the night—
and then again, found her here on the road home.

More than his voice, though. Yes, many voices.

Toward this you'll begin to walk in the pages someday—
pretending to merely translate them she said, mocking his fear as
he began to read her final letter in the notebook.

Easier this way.

Her father had turned to the other monks in the fields as
the soldiers' gunfire erupted around her. If she had been dying
then, she would have asked her father the same question. Though
she did not need to answer it now. The need to carry on? So you
spat, open your eyes. Oranges, tulips, a pencil!

All of this living spills into our love-stained mouths.

BACK IN EZEKIEL'S GARDEN

OF ALL THE EXPANSE THAT PASSED
THROUGH THEM, PETER SENSES THAT THIS DREAM
WILL BE THE MOST DIFFICULT, THE BOY TELLS THE
MONKS AT THE TABLE. FOR SHE IS SHOWING CER-
TAIN SIGNS IN HER FACE—THAT RAREFIED COUNTE-
NANCE. DEMURE OF A CHILD. A FACE OF DESIRE. THE
WAY SHE SWINGS HER LEGS CARELESSLY BENEATH
HER MOTHER'S BED. THE LAUGHTER OF HER BLACK
EYES EVEN SHEDDING THE ONCE DAMAGED SKIN
AND BEAUTY OF HER ACTUAL AGE IN YOUR
PAGES....IN THE GUISE OF A CHILD. THOUGH THIS OF
COURSE IS WHY HE HAS ALWAYS LOVED HER IS IT
NOT, EZEKIEL?

IT IS.

BUT SOMEDAY SHE WILL HAVE TO COME TO
US ON HER OWN, EZEKIEL REMINDS THE BOY, AND
RETURN OUR NOTEBOOKS.

day fifty three

   The story had no ending yet so much grief would be put
to rest. The search for ripe green apples. Walking in this way.
Walk in the sun. For who he might become. The image of her,
yes. Even when emaciated: beautiful. Where will he go? In the
beginning was the word. . . . An excess of horses on the road tonight.
The word made flesh? Or blown yellow leaves. Two tires lying in
the weeds. Walk in the sun. See the tracks to the east, a turning
point and then. Her hand going on there.
   This windmill.
   The boy waving from beyond the windmill.
   It could happen this way.

day fifty four

    When she came into his rented cottage the next night,
she no longer had a face. Not her face. Each hour had unfolded in
his hands like the hours of a clock as he waited. Not because of
the death but within it. Something you wanted to tell this other
person. Now, you can only tell yourself, he thinks. A conflict of
love. An encounter with the woman he can still touch, like the
hours, one from which everything—her hands, hair, teeth, eyes,
throat—are realized. A page of the body. Have you found the boy,
she laughed, entering the room, though he did not recognize her.
The hero of the story. As when the first day began. Fantastic, this
love. And that's enough. An angel came toward her, they touched,
and now, the man will always want her.

Dear Peter,

And so you see, it's been like this for centuries already.
Because we have planted these stories that have no time and pro-
vide no barriers between us. And so like your love, ours begins to
repeat and dissolve into another series of beginnings. Among these
waters and these fish. Outside of history. Our body. This word.
Yet this does not bother us, Peter. Like any soul, ours will eventu-
ally turn in on itself. If, that is, it's left alone long enough. And
we've been left alone, sufficiently alone, to wander this distance
with God. Simply on its own, the soul looks at the Face. Though
the things we see in the world we desire. If it knew how to tell
itself, the world wouldn't need us, or perhaps even care for all of
our journeys through these fields to find you. But it's clear. You
understand now. We dream of lovers, as lovers dream of us, and
somewhere the stories too are human. So we sip our tea and return
to reading the signs: the faces on the coins. Dreaming the day
when you will again fall from the sky. As if nothing has ever
occurred to impede this knowledge and absence. We've written
this story, but we can't resist it. Why should we, you will one day
ask? There are better things. Such as walking or singing or talking
to strangers, or falling from the sky. . . . The salt sits at the table
beside us today. Look at its blind eyes. Its ravaged mouth. its
desired body—its own wish to be retold and continue with each
plate of herring between each lover that ventures into you. We
can't help the attraction. Since the story has its own way of mak-
ing things available. This dream of you that has given evidence to
who we are. In this notebook of desire—our journal of walking.
Making all things alive, even beauty. Cockroaches, worms, words,
coins, skies—where past, present and future can be revealed. And
why not? The soul with its all beginning. You will come and you
will go, but this moment that ceases to be a moment, this hour

118

that ceases to be an hour, this word that ceases to be a word we may dream in the eyes of others. Eyes: the coins of God. Love's face. Even for those who refuse to come into your fields. We believe. Fishskins. Fisheyes. The chorus will sing them tonight. Sing them in this late snow of an afternoon too, as we await your next falling, and the cities around us burn. Yes, we are intimately aware of this joy. . . . The story turns its head and whistles. Now a whistle here, a whistle there. And on and on and on it goes, whistling.

Ezekiel's final letter to the apostle Peter, 987

THE WATER

Trying to reconstruct the events would be impossible. So
let memory have them. She had told him this as they walked
across the white beach. All that had been dead or thrown away
appeared in their gaunt movements. Blue slime, pestilence, mos-
quitoes, rain. The clarity of sun beating down. Nothing can ever
be reconstructed, you understand that, don't you? she went on,
shivering slightly as the waves began to touch her ankles, the hem
of her skirt.

Rock islands in the further distance. A beach, albino
gulls. It made one want to swim. He glanced back at her, but only
for a moment.

It's salt.

Yes, it's salty, she assured him.

And tomorrow?

Among the mosquitoes and earlier rain, the deltas of
black soil, it had been enough. Her image inhabited this place
where the fear had diminished. Why else had the soldiers put
down their rifles.

The water warm between his legs, easy to walk in. A flock
of pelicans fishing along the southern cliffs.

But who will tell our story? he asked.

Her glance leaving little to reckon. Can you see her? Her
senses at ease, shaped patterns on her wet arms and neck.

A canopy of fish, seaweed, floating algae. Or this sen-
tence. This background: examining the self and its sources; step-
ping in and out of their lives.

Each history was told before us. She smiled, looping his
elbow in her own elbow as the tide rose. Who could refuse these
singing mouths?

The Notebooks had given them this vision.

When the earth turned to salt and the skies came down
to meet the soldiers walking toward the sea.

Why do you ask about tomorrow? she whistled, splashing
the first of the water into his face. It was warm in my underarms.
The branch of a torn eucalyptus slid past us like a wooden boat.
They let it pass. He put his mouth on hers.

She opened her body.

Someone heard the singing, but who? She took his hand,
preparing for the subsequent walk that awaited them on the other
shore.

Where now then? he asked.

Floating into the source of these questions. An albatross
sits on one of the cliffs behind them. The narrow wings and large
hooked beak. The sea carried it here. The tide picks up the sol-
diers' rifles randomly strewn across the beach. The tide picks them
up. They carry out to sea. The albatross sits.

She remembers this now:

Her sun-burned face. They are almost laughing. No more
talking. Rock islands not as far away. A whitebacked angel on the
whitebacked rocks. The sleeping weeds.

The fishing pelicans. The two faces turning in the sun.
The waves allow each day to become its own.

The fishwoman with fish coming out of her mouth,
standing by the shoreline.

So many open mouths.

PETER

Just like the words of our first wanderer. So we arrive uncircumcised of heart? Into one more field, an eye. Everything is ready now. Wandering in and out of the pages as you watch the boy and his black crow walk toward the monastery. Answer the question then. Answer us with a smile which deserves the attention of my Achilles' feather pen. A story still flying toward absence and without a body and therefore without boundaries. We rub our hands over the fire and wait. The blackness of a blind eye, a raw mouth. When the wind starts. Comes alive again. Leaves you.

Siberia, 1995

from RAVAGE

Pai Chang also asked Wu Feng,"With your throat, mouth, and lips shut, how will you speak?"

Feng said, "Teacher, you too should shut up."

Chang said, "Where there's no one, I shade my eyes with my hand and gaze out towards you."

—*Blue Cliff Record*

Chao Chao Addresses The Assembly

The Word bends & curves and creates a life of its own, but eventually it comes home to you.

What is this mystery?

You find it residing in the furthermost channels of your cells, the blood, the very organs of a body.

Who are you if not this body?

The ghost comes home, as it has no other home, & eventually, no other place to go.

Have we renounced our own name then?

It does not reside in memory nor imagination, though the Word began here.

Absent in our presence?

The body is the only place deep enough to carry its resonance & fields of telling.

Who is this ghost?

The world is not what it is. It is what you are.

How is this our world? This is what I have come to ask.

I am no apostle, nor am I a ghost.

You are no longer one?

I am no longer an apostle, this is your world.

The word is dark, without sound?

Listen to the sound.

Yet a man walks down a long road for many years?

Look inside this man. The sky sees he is frightened, alone. You should help him, says the ghost.

You were once the man?

We cannot help him, the sky replies.

Where is the Word now?

Yet the man is destitute. You could make him wealthy, the ghosted one says.

I am the ghost?

A god takes a bag of gold & drops it from the heavens around the bend of the road the man is walking.

I am that man?

As the man trudges on with the others, his eyes are cast downward.

Who is the traveler among many?

Not seeing the bag of gold, the man's foot strikes it & he lets out a deep wail.

I know only the man's laughter.

You see he is tired. The laughter is a wail & the man walks around the bag of gold.

Have I met this ghost?

Let me tell you a story.

I am sick of words.

Another ravaged one comes alas to a master. He says--My life is ravage.

Where is our ravage?

The master reaches inside her eyes. You have already tasted three glasses of the finest wine, she says.

Am I drunk then?

Since the master understood the ravage brought love into the quest.

Where is the woman?

You have drunk three glasses of the finest wine.

Are you the one who speaks of names?

The mind seeks a name.

In our name is only a story?

You are once a word, a ghost, & a story.

Why have we come then?

We arrived together. Still the Word is lonely, consumed, ravaged.

How can I help them?

You are the only master.

Have I mastered no word?

You seek no other.

Though I have known the life of a child.

We are the life of a child.

The taste of the woman is still in my mouth?

You behold no other.

Have I come without a gift?

Awe is before us.

Where can we go?

This is a good place for a temple.

We are not builders of temples.

Pluck a leaf of grass, scoop a small piece of earth into the hands, place the leaf into the very ground.

What is this earth?

No one else speaks before you.

Why do you not speak our Name?

We have been so since the Beginning.

Can you give us no other sign?

You seek signs when you already touch the sex.

Ravage?

And before you a body of mouths, three glasses of the finest wine, a complete treasure.

To what end?

Yet the wail is a shadow is laughter in the dream.

Unawakened, yes. You call the self a word?

What else would you expect from a story, if not for it to change your very life.

Whose mouth has spoken?

And if I answered you, would you still not know the voice?

Designed by
Samuel Retsov

Text: 12 pt Baskerville Old Face

acid-free paper

Printed by
McNaughton & Gunn